The Key
to
Mexico

REG BUTLER

In Association with

THOMSON HOLIDAYS

SETTLE PRESS

Text © 1996 Reg Butler

First published by Settle Press
10 Boyne Terrace Mews
London W11 3LR

ISBN (Paperback) 1 872876 43 9

Printed by Villiers Publications
19 Sylvan Avenue
London N3 2LE
Maps by Mary Butler

Foreword

As Britain's leading holiday company operating to the Caribbean, Thomson are happy to be associated with Reg Butler's new book 'The Key to Mexico'. In writing the book, the author worked closely with our resident representatives and local agents who have year-round contact with holiday-makers' travel interests.

Whether you have chosen to stay on the Caribbean or the Pacific Coast, we feel this pocket book can act as a quick reference guide to the sightseeing potential beyond the beaches.

It's impossible to see everything in two or three weeks. When the holiday is over, we suggest you keep this guide-book to help plan your return visit - perhaps to the other coast which you did not have time to explore.

All prices mentioned in the text were accurate at the time of printing. But Mexico has an inflation problem, and local prices will certainly change during the coming year. However, any costs quoted in the book can serve as guidance to the average level of expenses.

THOMSON HOLIDAYS

Contents

Chapter One

Be conquered by Mexico

The tourist slogan says it all: Let yourself be conquered by Mexico. The country offers a stunning range of seductive attractions. The warm climate, friendly people, fiesta spirit, Latin lifestyle, music, culture and history all combine to make an easy surrender to the charms of Mexico.

There's so much to see and do. For British visitors it's hard to imagine the sheer size of the country. Mexico's area is 760,000 square miles. That's the size of Britain, France, Spain, Germany and Italy together.

Mexico is bordered by four seas – the Pacific Ocean, the Gulf of Mexico, the Sea of Cortés, the Caribbean – with 5,800 miles of coastline.

Gorgeous sandy beaches await sun worshippers and watersport enthusiasts. Mexico has developed a great reputation as a diver's paradise, for exploring marine life in waters where visibility exceeds 50 feet.

That is especially true around the islands of Cozumel and Isla Mujeres, and along the entire coast accessible from Cancún. Palancar Reef is ranked by scuba divers as among the world's finest, six miles long and 3000 feet deep. The potential was revealed by Jacques Cousteau in his underwater films that became so popular on TV.

Divers can mingle with multi-coloured tropical fish. Equipment can easily be rented, and many hotels and dive shops offer training courses. The marine delights are also open to snorkellers, while glass-bottom boats and a submarine await those who prefer to admire fish without getting their feet wet.

Inland there is great variety of landscape. Snow-capped mountains and extinct volcanoes dwarf the Alps. They act as an awesome backdrop to the high plateaux, deep gorges and desert areas. Nearly half the country is more than 5000 feet above sea level.

In contrast, the Yucatán Peninsula is low-lying and flat, covered in a tangled jungle. Here, 2000 years ago, Mayan temples and cities were built of a grandeur that could rival anything in Europe. Great pyramids and observatories were constructed, based on a calendar much more accurate than the Julian calendar of the Romans. In mathematics they were centuries ahead of the Western world.

The Yucatán's natural heritage continues to thrive in extensive reserves that comprise rain forest, coral reef and lagoon habitats. Descendants of the Mayan people still plant maize, beans and squash, the food of their ancestors.

When the Spaniards marched into the heart of Mexico in early 16th century, they marvelled at the Aztec capital which they described as more beautiful than anywhere in Spain.

But the temple pyramids were pagan. They were soon demolished along with Aztec palaces and other monuments, to be recycled into churches, Colonial mansions and public buildings. The original Aztec site is today's Mexico City, with the world's largest population edging towards twenty million.

In their quest for riches, the Spaniards found that silver paid off better than gold. The Colonial cities of the central plateau ploughed part of their prosperity into elegant mansions, monasteries and churches, focussed on a central plaza.

By the early 19th century, the cry was for independence from Spain. Many of the Colonial cities erupted, to leave their mark on history.

Festivals

The Mexicans are Catholic, but sometimes only in a nominal sense. They go to church on social occasions like baptisms, weddings or burials, with a party to follow after each of these events.

The calendar is filled with local church and secular festivals, with good excuse for song and dance and fiesta costume. Local traditions give each event its own special texture. It's worth a long drive, to participate first-hand.

On the beach

Whichever coast of Mexico you choose for a beach holiday, Caribbean or Pacific, there is great potential for holiday pleasure.

Throughout the day there's choice between dreamy relaxation, the more active land-based or water sports, sightseeing or shopping. Even the most dedicated non-shopper can enjoy the downtown Flea Markets with light-hearted haggling for colourful Mexican giftware.

At sunset the nightlife begins, with most bars offering a Happy Hour of two drinks for the price of one. Happy Hour can stretch through half the evening. A bar in Puerto Vallarta even proclaims "Happy Hour 24 hours a day."

Catering for every taste, discos, bars and restaurants line the hotel zones and downtown areas, while the larger hotels and all-inclusive resorts feature their own evening entertainment with international or Mexican bands.

By all means enjoy the beaches and the nightlife. But try to make time for some of the sightseeing highlights. Of course, on a two- or three-week holiday, a visitor can only skim the surface of Mexico's rich heritage of the past 2,000 years. But it's still worth making your own discoveries.

In this "Key to Mexico" we open the door to a brief cross-section of the country's great treasures: history, culture, music, dance, scenery, romantic cities, cuisine and smiling, friendly people. Let yourself be conquered.

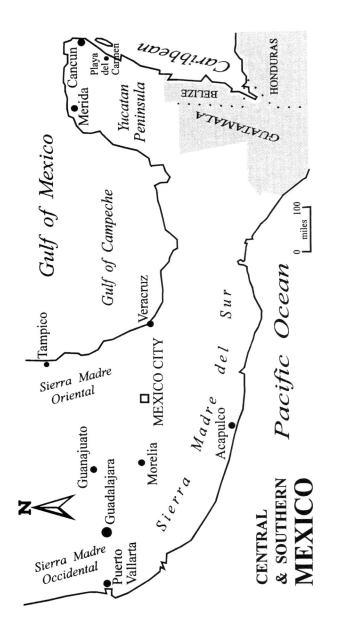

CENTRAL
& SOUTHERN
MEXICO

Chapter Two

Planning to go

2.1 Which season?

Mexican resorts offer two weather seasons: rainy summer and dry winter. Midday temperatures range in the 80s and 90s. Winter months are the best time to go. However, even during summer, the rainfall tends to come in short, heavy downpours; and then the sun dries it up.

The sun rises about 5.30 a.m. and sets year-round between 5.30 and 6.00 p.m. Rain comes mostly around sunset.

2.2 Money matters

Local currency is the New Peso, usually written as N\$, which splits into 100 centavos. Old peso banknotes with lots of zeroes have been withdrawn, and are rarely seen (they were converted at 1,000 to one).

The principal coins are 1, 2, 5 and 10 pesos. Banknotes are for 10, 20, 50, 100, 200 and 500 pesos. You can recognise old currency by the number of zeroes. If a peso note has two or more zeroes, check it out very carefully.

The New Peso is a more realistic currency, though its value has been plunging since devaluation in December 1994. Check the current exchange rate before leaving home.

The US dollar is the most powerful currency, and many prices are quoted in dollars – car hire and excursions, for instance, or even set meals. Many market traders will only talk dollars.

Visitors from Britain should bring US bank-notes and dollar traveller cheques. Exchange rates for sterling or any other European currency are very poor when compared with dollars. Scottish or Irish currency are virtually impossible to exchange. Just swallow any national pride in sterling, and accept that in Mexico the US dollar is king.

Even with dollars, it's worth shopping for better exchange rates. For best rates, go to regular banks, though they are open mornings only and you may have to queue. Next best are the exchange kiosks, especially in downtown areas. Most hotels are less generous. Worst of all are the exchange desks at the arrival airport – those at Cancún airport are a rip-off, unless they have since reformed. Shops and restaurants will accept dollars, but mostly they convert at rates that improve their profit margins.

Major credit cards have wide acceptance. *But don't rely too heavily on plastic, as many of these transactions are loaded with a 6% bank fee to agents for processing. Check first!*

How much spending money?

Obviously this depends on what activities you plan. The main resorts are not as cheap as the rest of Mexico, but nor are they overpriced. They are cheaper than most Caribbean islands, except for the Dominican Republic or Jamaica.

Take enough funds so that you don't miss the spectacular excursions and nights out. If you have chosen an all-inclusive resort, then your meals, drinks, most sport facilities and entertainment are covered. But don't forget to budget for tours or car hire.

For holidaymakers at non-inclusive hotels, eating out is about the same cost as London, but cheaper if you head downtown to sample more local cuisine.

Shopping is cheap for local products, but with no bargains for imported luxury items.

2.3 *Arrival formalities*

Immigration officials just take a quick glance at European passports, with no visa needed. Visitors are given a Tourist Card which must be turned in upon leaving Mexico.

An exit tax is charged on departure, payable in dollars or pesos. Thomson Holidays include this tax in their package price.

A Customs declaration is required on arrival, with random inspection of baggage. Trolleys can be hired for a dollar. En route to your tour bus, ignore the porters who pretend to be the company's employees, each expecting a hefty tip. For individual travellers there are shared limousine services which deliver you to your hotel at a low-cost set tariff, with no haggling or tipping.

2.4 *What to pack*

Resort wear is casual – light tops or T-shirts, sandals, shorts; jeans for the evening. Some discos will not allow you to enter wearing shorts or trainers. Otherwise, travel out light on clothing, as Mexico has plentiful dress bargains to make happy shopping.

Swimsuits are for the beach or pool area only, as modesty is expected when walking around shops or hotels. European-style topless sun-bathing is not forbidden, but keep a modest distance from shockable hotel guests who may come from less liberated cultures. Americans in particular feel uncomfortable with this European custom.

If you expect to visit Mexico City, pack a sweater or light jacket. Daytime temperatures can be very pleasant, but nights turn chilly. The capital's dress code is somewhat more formal, so pack a tie for dining in up-market restaurants.

When visiting churches, ladies should take a head-scarf. It's also advisable to take trousers, as some priests frown upon shorts or mini-skirts. Trousers and trainers or hard-soled sandals are best for jungle and archaeological trips.

13

2.5 Health and medicine

Too much alcohol, spicy food and hot sun can lead to upset stomachs. Be cautious and follow a policy of moderation during the first few days.

The local water is rarely to blame. All the main resort restaurants and hotels use purified water, and ice cubes are safe. Tap water is also purified, though not entirely up to EC standards. For total caution, buy bottled water. But it's not really necessary except in remote areas.

Far more important is to be well armed against the tropical sun. Start with a protection factor of 15 or 20, and read the instructions on the bottle, twenty minutes on either side. Remember that the sun's rays penetrate palapa roofs, they go through water, and can burn even through cloud.

There is no malaria in the Mexican resorts or principal cities, so there's no need for anti-malaria tablets. However there are lots of mosquitoes. They emerge at sunset, and normally finish supper by about 9 p.m.

Come prepared with suitable repellant sprays and creams. To ensure peaceful sleep, shut bedroom windows before dusk and leave the air conditioning switched on.

Most hotels fumigate rooms regularly, to discourage other insects. Vacate your room for a couple of hours until the insecticide has settled. In hotels which are on the edge of the jungle – like those at Playa del Carmen – they also fumigate outside, to discourage spiders and snakes.

All major towns and resorts have good medical facilities and pharmacies, but bring a full supply of any medicine that you use regularly.

In case of illness, rest assured that resort doctors are some of the best trained in the world, and are on permanent call. Mostly they have qualified in Costa Rica, where training standards are high. Medical practice is private. Fees and the cost of any medication can be reclaimed from insurance on return to Britain, subject to what your policy permits.

2.6 Wedding plans

If you are planning to get married in Mexico, blood tests are a legal requirement, and must be done in Mexico. The prices of blood tests vary, from between 50 and 70 US dollars per couple. Guests can be completely confident that any clinic that is used will be of the highest standard, and with the use of sterile needles.

The normal recommendation is to have blood tests done on the day after arrival, or as soon as possible. It's best not to eat or drink prior to the tests, so make an early appointment.

Arrangements for the wedding will vary, depending on the hotel in which the couple are staying. The basic reservations for the service will already be made, and all other details can be agreed on arrival: style of wedding cake, bride's bouquet, wines. Sparkling wines are reasonably priced. Real champagne can cost £60 upwards.

The ceremonies are conducted in Spanish, though an English translation can be arranged. A service normally takes about 20 minutes, and is a much more joyous affair than in the traditional UK registry office. The wedding location can be decorated with flowers and balloons, or in Mexican style with coloured blankets and sombreros. There's great applause from onlookers when the bride arrives escorted by optional musicians.

The time of day for the ceremony is very important. By 10 a.m. it's like midsummer high noon in the Mediterranean – not the ideal time for getting married in full wedding dress.

A late afternoon ceremony ensures better lighting for good quality photographs. Celebrations can then continue through the evening, rather than having a morning wedding and jumping into the swimming pool half an hour later.

Chapter Three

The Caribbean coastline

3.1 Beaches by computer

Around 1970 the Mexican government completed a project study to select the most perfect location for a major new resort along the Caribbean coast.

All the major ingredients were already in place: many miles of superb sands composed of finely powdered shells, limestone and coral; year-round sunshine refreshed by sea breezes; the world's second longest coral reef after the Great Barrier Reef of Australia; total absence of industrial pollution; proximity to historic archaeological sites.

The computer choice was a 14-mile island strip, shaped like a figure '7', which enclosed a beautiful lagoon on the eastern coast of the Yucatán Peninsula.

Along that entire length were fabulous white beaches, soft as talcum powder. Water sports could operate in the Caribbean itself, or in the more placid waters of the lagoon. There was even potential for a high-grade golf course or two.

In this location untouched by man, the nearest settlement was the tiny fishing village of Puerto Juárez. The island was designated as a Hotel Zone, totally reserved for holiday development, and connected by a bridge each end to the mainland, where the separate downtown area of Cancún was sited.

Programmed for pleasure
Actual building started in 1972, and the first hotel opened in 1974. Since then, every tourist service has been fully developed: hotels, time-share apartments, restaurants and bars, glitzy shopping malls and sparkling nightlife.

New highways through the jungle offer day-trip access to the highlights of the Yucatán Peninsula – to the incredible Mayan sites which formerly were difficult to reach.

Cancún now rates as Mexico's leading holiday destination. From an initial population of 300 people, Cancún City itself has grown to over 300,000.

South of Cancún, several smaller resorts have arisen. The most important is Playa del Carmen – originally a fishing village offering access to Cozumel island. Now it's a laid-back resort with a Mediterranean atmosphere, in contrast to the American style of Cancún's Hotel Zone.

3.2 Arrival – orientation

The air approach to Cancún is dramatic: first the green coastal jungle, and then the grid-pattern streets of Cancún centre, Mexico's newest township.

The aircraft sweeps past the huge lagoon, offering a pelican's-eye view of the Hotel Zone. The international luxury palaces are silhouetted like cruising battleships, line astern along the waterfront.

The surrounding waters are visibly a scuba-divers' paradise, every shade of green and blue that indicates the varying depth of the waters and the presence of coral reefs.

The airport is not a great international giant, but middle-size and friendly. The immigration and customs officials welcome visitors with a smile. Cancún's Hotel Zone is only a short distance away; or about a 40-minute drive to Playa del Carmen. After the long haul from Europe, relaxation is close at hand.

Finding your way

Orientation in the Hotel Zone couldn't be simpler. Everything is spread along the 14-mile Kukulcán Boulevard (named after the Mayan sun god), with a distance marker at every half kilometre. These markers are useful for locating a particular hotel or restaurant, as the kilometre location becomes part of the address.

There's water on both sides of the highway: the Caribbean on one side, and Laguna Nichupté on the other. The broad dual carriageway is lined with shady palm trees.

Cycle paths are used by joggers and rollerbladers. Major activities are focussed around the Convention Center, where the island bends into its figure-7 shape.

Bus transport is excellent: very frequent and with a standard fare of about 30p any distance – end to end of the Boulevard and across the bridge to the centre of Cancún town. The very obliging drivers will often stop even between the official stages.

Taxis cruise the boulevard, and swoop into the hotel forecourt if they see you standing. Cabs are not metered, but use a set tariff according to a zonal system.

3.3 Cancún

Downtown is made up of four principal avenues, named after Mayan sites: Tulum and Yaxchilan, which run north to south, and Uxmal and Cobá, which run east to west. Alight from your bus at the roundabout with starfish sculptures and gushing fountains.

In this central location, the streets are lined with tourist shops, supermarkets, and dozens of excellent restaurants that serve Mexican cuisine. All prices are lower than in the Hotel Zone, especially if you explore the side streets. Keen shoppers can haggle for Mexican giftware in the so-called Flea Market in a maze just off Tulum Avenue.

3.4 Isla Mujeres

Facing Cancún, Isla Mujeres is a long thin island, shaped like a fish, four miles long and 1,300 feet wide. Appropriately, sea-food is the speciality of the local restaurants. Former fishermen are almost entirely involved in watersport tourism and its spinoffs.

Access is easy, with frequent boats that ply from Playa Linda and other locations in Cancún's Hotel Zone, or by public half-hourly ferry services from Puerto Juárez. Arrivals at the tourist pier are watched by resident pelicans. Soft sand at the harbour is a foretaste of good beaches elsewhere around the island. Buildings on the waterfront and in the side streets are brightly painted and prosperous. Shops sell everything from high-grade jewellery to hammocks and Mayan figurines.

Luxury cruisers arrive for a fun day around the island, for enjoyment of the serene atmosphere, snorkelling and scuba-diving, with lunch and open bar included. Another regular service is operated aboard the supposed replica of a Spanish galleon, which is equipped with decorated sails and a diesel engine.

Individual travellers can tour the island by renting a bicycle, moped, Volkswagen or golf cart. Topless sunbathing is accepted at Playa Norte, which is often pronounced as Naughty Beach, spelt Nautibeach.

The island was first called the 'Island of Women' when Spaniards landed in 1518, and found numerous Mayan female clay figurines that were fertility symbols. Later the island became like a rest centre for pirates and slave traders. But no trace remains from those wild times.

Today, a big attraction is to snorkel or scuba-dive in the reef area of El Garrafón Bay, teeming with any parrotfish and angelfish who haven't been scared off by shoals of snorkellers. For more expert scuba divers, there's a 68-foot dive into a renowned Cave of the Sleeping Sharks.

3.5 *Playa del Carmen*

Regular buses ply between Playa del Carmen and Cancún at around £1 for the 42-mile journey. Originally a small fishing village, Playa del Carmen is an up-and-coming resort which maintains its Mexican charm. Beaches are fabulous and offer plenty of watersports. Frequent ferries ply to the island of Cozumel, 12 miles offshore.

Main Street is Avenida 5A Norte, pedestrianized in the centre, with full shopping choice of clothes, arts, crafts and jewellery. At night there's a delightful cosmopolitan air among the pavement cafés and restaurants where customers drink enormous Margaritas and other cocktails served in large goblets like goldfish bowls. For late-night people there are two discos, but many bars have dancing and late music.

Even for residents at an all-inclusive complex, there's good reason to get out and enjoy the local scene and its serenity. People-watching is a great pastime, with a constant flow of international oddities from backpackers to trendy European jet-setters. But you can still feel much closer to Mexico than is possible in Cancún.

3.6 *Dive off to Cozumel*

For anyone staying at Playa del Carmen, it's simple to take a ferry across to Cozumel and explore the island and its beaches. Guests at the Caribbean Village and the Diamond Resort can enjoy reciprocal facilities at Diamond Hotel in the same group.

It's easy to do one's own thing. Haggle away and charter a taxi to tour the island, go snorkelling or diving. It costs only a few dollars from the Diamond to the Chankanaab National Park, which is a beautiful natural aquarium with beach and coral reef. Schools of yellow and black sergeant majors dart amid the coral formations.

Ranking as Mexico's finest for scuba-diving sites, Cozumel has become famous since Jacques

Cousteau explored the Palancar Reef, which is listed among the world's greatest.

The island, 24 miles long, is generally flat with dense jungle filling the interior. Beaches are pounded by rough surf on the eastward side, but waters are calmer facing the mainland.

Because less than five percent of the island is developed, wildlife and marine life flourish on and around Cozumel. The jungle shelters herons, iguanas, egrets and armadillos. During July, nature lovers watch as baby sea turtles, raised in a local hatchery, are released and make their way down the beach to swim freely for the first time.

In San Miguel, where most of the 60,000 island residents live, the streets are lined with tourist shops. Some restaurants serve traditional Mayan dishes such as *pollo pibil* and *tikin-xik* (chicken and fish dishes).

From Cancún full day tours are operated to Cozumel. Ask your tour rep for the latest prices.

3.7 Take a trip

A full range of day excursions, by sea or land, are operated from Cancún. See the next chapter for visits to the archaeological sites of the Yucatán – to Chichén Itzá, Tulum and Cobá. As mentioned above, there's wide choice of day and night trips to Isla Mujeres, and also an all-day package to Cozumel.

If you're not a dedicated scuba-diver, it's a great experiences to visit the seabed by submarine. The craft used is a real submarine, not a Walt Disney prototype. From Playa Linda you are ferried 20 minutes out to sea, and are then down-loaded into the waiting submarine for a fisheye view of the seabed and its marine life.

Cruising for an hour, submerged between 35 and 50 feet below sea level, the submarine visits natural and man-made reefs. Professional divers feed fish, to encourage them close to the portholes. Photography is possible with a fast film, like 400 ASA. In clear water on a good sunny day, there's enough light. Otherwise try a slower shutter speed. But don't use flash, which bounces back from the glass.

An alternative trip at Cancún is aboard the Sub Sea Viewer – a catamaran with glass panels in the keels, at eye level with the fish.

Tourist corridor

South along Highway 307 from Cancún, the 80-mile stretch of coast is known as the Cancún-Tulum Corridor. The road, running inland but parallel to the coast, passes through low tangled jungle, linking the diversity of Cancún or Playa del Carmen to the mysteries of the Mayan ruins of Tulum.

En route are bumpy turn-offs to smaller resorts like Puerto Morelos, Puerto Aventuras and Akumal – besides a number of Robinson Crusoe beaches like Punta Bete, down a long dirt track leading to a wonderful fish restaurant. There's great potential for beach-lovers and snorkellers, with several nature-based attractions along the way.

There is good choice of guided coach tours, linking two or three of the main attractions, such as Tulum with snorkelling at Akumal. Otherwise, car hire is the best option for total independence. Avoid returning after dark, as truck drivers can make the narrow road hazardous. Also, when passing through any inhabited area, slow right down for the traffic-calming bumps.

Attractions

Here's a summary of the main points of interest. Note that any entrance prices are quoted for rough guidance, but are likely to change through inflation and devaluation.

Palancar Aquarium is located 20 miles south of Cancún, with exhibits on the area's marine life and environment.

Croco Cun is a crocodile farm next door, where American crocodiles and Central American caymans are reared by taking newly laid eggs and hatching them in temperature controlled rooms. The breeding station features more than 300 reptiles in walled ponds. Open 8-18 hrs, entrance about £2.

Dr. Alfredo Barrera Marín Botanical Garden is just outside Puerto Morelos, and features local flora labelled in Spanish, a nature trail and a small archaeological site.

Puerto Morelos is a very peaceful resort giving access to favoured coral reefs, with caverns and multicoloured marine life. In former times, this was the departure point for Mayan women making pilgrimages to Cozumel.

Punta Bete is a gorgeous beach edged with coconut trees.

Playa del Carmen – see details above.

Xcaret is an ecological theme park that combines Mayan ruins with coves, inlets, horseback riding, jungle trails and cenotes. The park's main attraction is an underground river ride. Visitors are fitted with life jacket and snorkel, to float gently for 1,700 feet through caverns with multi-hued fish. You can book to swim with captive dolphins, first come first served, but very expensive.

Open daily, Xcaret is 45 miles south of Cancún or 4 miles from Playa del Carmen. Entrance about £12.

Puerto Aventuras is a 980-acre self-contained resort with a 250-boat slip, private villas, a 9-hole Golf Course, a beach club and dive centre.

CEDAM Underwater Archaeology Museum displays artifacts collected from a Spanish merchant ship that sank in 1741. Exhibits include belt buckles, cannons, coins, guns, tableware and various clay relics from Mayan ruins along the Quintana Roo coast. Admission free.

Akumal, 22 miles south of Playa del Carmen, is a charming beach greatly favoured by snorkellers and divers. The northern palm-lined area, formerly a coconut plantation, is known as Half Moon Bay. A small Mayan community offers their wares at informal markets. Several lesser-known beaches in the area are worth a visit, including **Playa Chemuyil** and **Xcacel**.

Xel-Há is a National Park, ten acres of stunning lagoons, coves and inlets carved by nature into the soft limestone. The Quintana Roo coast offers many wonderful snorkel options for experts and beginners alike. But Xel-Ha is quite outstanding, a natural aquarium teeming with tropical fish.

Ten miles south of Akumal, Xel-Ha features underwater caves, *cenotes* (sinkholes) and a partially submerged Mayan ruin. Rent snorkel gear, or visit the far side of the lagoon by glass-bottom boats. Xel-Ha also includes a shrine, a maritime museum and a seafood restaurant. Open daily, admission £3.

Tulum – see next chapter.

Sian Ka'an Biosphere Reserve, past Tulum, is a 1,300,000-acre wilderness area established in 1986, comprising tropical forests, wetlands and marine environments.

In scattered islets are nesting sites for water birds including woodstorks, frigate birds and boat-billed herons. Rare jabiru storks nest in the reserve, and the beaches are nesting grounds for endangered sea turtles. Shallow bays comprise Mexico's most important spiny lobster nursery.

Among the protected species are manatee, monkeys, jaguars, ocelots and crocodiles. Approximately 1,200 plant species also are found in the area. Fewer than 1,000 people, mostly Mayan fishermen and farmers, inhabit the buffer zones of the reserve.

3.8 All the sports

Swimming – All beaches are public, so you can swim anywhere. But it's advisable to stay in selected swimming areas. Some parts of Cancún's beach are especially good for surfing, while others are flat as a lake. In some locations, undercurrents can be dangerous. Listen to any advice given by suppliers of water sports.

Take heed of beach flags. Green is OK, yellow for caution, red for danger except for good swimmers, and black for no swimming permitted. Check before taking the plunge.

You can sample other hotels and use their beaches, except for the all-inclusive properties where guests are identified by a bracelet tag.

Caution: during May and June, the Caribbean coast is sometimes visited by thimble fish. These are tiny jelly fish, the size of a two pence piece, transparent and almost invisible. They are attracted to Lycra. Sea bathers in Lycra costumes can get thimble fish trapped inside their swimsuits. The thimble fish are not felt in the water. But the swimmer will be covered on bottom and breasts with prickling weals, the brown marks of the jellyfish. So check before swimming during those two months.

The best cure is a rapid shower to remove the jellyfish from your swimwear and your body. Locals say that vinegar helps. But if you have been bitten badly, call a doctor immediately.

Water sports – The Caribbean coast is heaven for snorkellers and scuba-divers. For non-divers who would like a trial run, most of the inclusive hotels offer a free one-hour introductory dive. This first lesson is given in the hotel swimming pool, just to accustom beginners to being underwater, and to teach the basic techniques.

Anyone who wants to plunge deeper can then book a full diving course. Diving instruction and gear don't come cheap, but a course opens up the fabulous world of underwater life. For divers who are already qualified, dive shops show video tapes of sites that can be explored. These are not only natural sea dives, but also inland cave dives in cenotes or sink holes.

There is wide choice of every other water sport: deep-sea and shore fishing, kayaking, windsurfing, water-skiing, sailing (sunfish, Hobie

Cat), jetskiing and parasailing. Some activities may be included or arranged through your hotel, but varied beach and marina enterprises also offer these services.

Dolphins – In several locations people can swim with semi-captive dolphins. The experience will cost $60 to $70 on top of any normal tour cost. Despite the price, it's essential to book up immediately on arrival. At Xcaret, for instance, only 36 people a day can be accepted for a swim. During high season, people arrive early and queue to get themselves booked in.

Horse riding – There is choice of beach or jungle horseback riding, costing $25 to $30 for a ride. The horses are quite a different breed from those used by stables in UK. A caution: hard hats are not provided, so pack your own.

Golf – Cancún has two excellent golf courses. Pok-Ta-Pok was designed by Robert Trent-Jones. Named after the ancient Mayan ball game, Pok--Ta-Pok borders on two exquisite deep blue lagoons that become part of the challenge. At the 12th hole, golfers must navigate a Mayan ruin that bisects the fairway. Green fees are $85, including a golf trolley. The course at Caesar's Park is even more expensive.

There is better value at Playa del Carmen, where the Playacar complex includes a superb course, beautifully landscaped with lakes and fountains, and an excellent club house. Residents at the Caribbean Village or the Diamond Resort get special concessionary rates for green fees, hire of clubs and trolley. For non-residents, the price is around $90.

Spectator sports – In addition to baseball, jai alai, dog and horse racing, there are many sport-related special events and competitions throughout the year.

3.9 Nightlife

At sunset Cancún switches into high-gear night-life that begins with Happy Hour and a good meal, followed by a sampling of every style of musical rhythm – from reggae and rock 'n roll to Latin and Caribbean tunes and sexy jazz. People dance, listen or just relax with a drink.

One of the main nightlife centres is focussed around the Hard Rock Cafe facing the Mayfair Shopping Mall and the bottom end of Caracol Plaza. It's a very lively restaurant and bar section, with nightlife sounding off until the small hours.

On a more cultural level is the dinner, open bar and show called 'Taste of Mexico', daily except Sunday, costing around £30; or half that with drinks only, at tables further from the stage. This show has been running for several years at the Continental Villas Plaza, featuring the National Folkloric Ballet of Mexico.

The two-hour performance opens with an evocation of ancient dance rituals from the mists of time, and continues with all the colourful variety of Mexican folk dancing and music, with authentic costumes from a dozen different regions. This famous ballet company has four groups – one performing regularly in Mexico City, and another travelling constantly worldwide as an ambassador of Mexican culture. Don't miss it!

A younger rival group is The Folkloric Ballet of Cancún which offers a much shorter programme at the Convention Center, with forty musicians and twenty vibrant dancers.

Afloat there is choice of night fiesta cruises, with buffet dinner, open bar, dancing and mariachi music. It's a great chance to live it up in Latin style, for a Mexican night to remember.

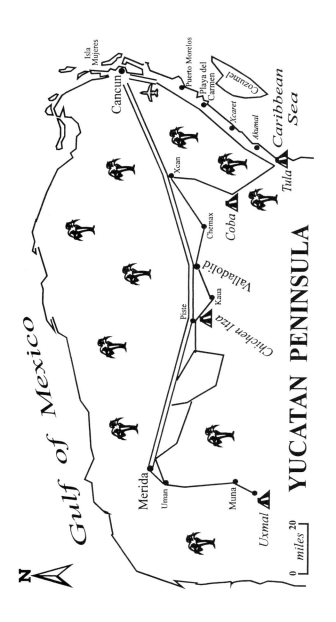

YUCATAN PENINSULA

Gulf of Mexico

Caribbean Sea

Isla Mujeres
Cancun
Puerto Morelos
Playa del Carmen
Cozumel
Xcaret
Akumal
Xcan
Tula
Coba
Chemax
Valladolid
Kaua
Piste
Chichen Itza
Merida
Uman
Muna
Uxmal

N

0   miles   20

Chapter Four

Gateway to the Yucatán

4.1 Introducing the Mayas

From 800 BC onwards the Yucatán Peninsula, and neighbouring countries to the south, saw development of an advanced Mayan civilization. Scattered settlements merged into centralised cities that became highly skilled in science and invention. Mayan mathematicians used today's concept of zero and a place-value system of numeration, long before similar ideas evolved in Europe. The Mayan calendar, based on precise astronomy, accurately measured the solar year and could project dates thousands of years in the past or into the future.

Cities and ceremonial centres blossomed especially in the Classic Period, between 250 and 900 AD, with planned urban layouts, broad boulevards, efficient water and sewage systems, great pyramids and palaces.

Brilliance in the sciences and in social structure was matched by artistic skills. Intricately crafted statues, wall carvings, paintings and abstract decorations set Mayan sites apart from those of any other world culture. Music and dance were used in religious ceremonies, employing a wide range of musical instruments. Yet curiously the Mayas never made use of the wheel (except in toys) or of domestic animals.

Mayan culture peaked around 900 AD and then declined rapidly. When the Spaniards arrived in the 16th century, the greatest Mayan cities had long been abandoned. The causes of the decline and fall remain a mystery, though theories abound.

Despite centuries of invasion, conquest, slavery and cultural deprivation, over 4,000,000 native speakers of Mayan languages still live in south eastern Mexico, Guatamala and parts of Belize, El Salvador and Honduras.

About 700,000 Mayas today inhabit the Yucatán Peninsula. To some extent they still preserve their pre-Hispanic and particularly Colonial and 19th-century customs. In recent times, they have played an increasing role in politics, especially in defence of their ethnic identity. They seek access to national life without losing their own culture.

Guided tours of the archaeological sites of Yucatán can also give an overview of today's Mayan lifestyle. Speed bumps at every village ensure that travellers get a slow look at peasant houses that comprise one main living-room, in which hammocks are strung across at night. Cooking is done in an outdoor kitchen. Little gardens are surrounded by walls of rough limestone, with free-range dogs and chickens.

Water supplies are pure, coming from underground streams which have filtered through layers of limestone bedrock. Likewise in classic times, settlements and religious sites were focussed on the cenotes or sink-holes which provided crystal-clear water.

Many farming techniques are unchanged from 2,000 years ago. Maize, beans and squash are sown together. The squash provides ground cover, while the beans twine up the maize stalks. The system works well in this region which has only about ten inches of poor soil above the limestone base. Slash-and-burn methods are still used in jungle clearings, with ashes fertilizing the soil until cultivation has to move on elsewhere. Ceremonies in honour of Chaac the Rain God are held on key dates according to the traditional planting calendar.

Up a gum tree

Cash income formerly came from forest products, including the 19th-century discovery of chicle resin from sapodilla trees, the original source for chewing gum. Honey still remains a big export. Sisal was important until markets were lost. The fibre is now used principally for making hammocks.

In recent years, men and women have found employment as home-based outworkers in the garments industry, especially in production of snow-white embroidered dresses called *huipiles*. Traditional crafts still flourish, including palm weaving, marquetry and working in tortoiseshell and snakeskin.

4.2 Chichén Itzá

If you're not making a full Yucatán highlights tour, the first choice from Cancún or Playa del Carmen should definitely be Chichén Itzá, though it's a long all-day trip to this great Mayan site. The Cancún-Mérida toll Highway 180, opened in 1993, makes the journey much easier than in former times, avoiding villages and speed bumps. Through the tortilla-flat jungle with no sign of human settlement, the green roadside teems with butterflies. Vultures glide overhead, alert for lunch.

A halt can be made in the colonial city of Vallodolid, an important market centre halfway between Cancún and Mérida. Its cathedral is claimed to be the second oldest in North America. Built in mid-16th century, it stands on the site of a Mayan temple which contributed the building materials.

The City Hall, several ancient churches and colonial houses are likewise recycled from Mayan monuments. The central plaza is charming, with white love seats designed so that courting couples could flirt face-to-face but without physical contact. The seats are still used for this purpose on Sundays.

The pyramid calendar

In a scrub jungle setting, 29 miles away, is Chichén Itzá. The world-famous remains are listed by UNESCO as a World Heritage Site. The awesome centrepiece is the temple pyramid dedicated to Kukulkán, the Plumed Serpent, also known to the Toltec people as Quetzalcóatl.

The four-sided pyramid doubled as a calendar in stone, with 91 steps each side, plus one last step to make a 365-day year.

If you clamber to the top, the reward is a magnificent view of the whole archaeological site. But take care! Like the pyramids in other sites, each step is very steep, with a very narrow pitch which entails a nerve-racking descent. Check how you feel, before going too high. Many visitors clamber down on all fours, or get help from a rope or chain.

On spring and autumn equinoxes – March 21 and September 21 – the sun casts a shadow that seems like a giant serpent slithering down the pyramid's steps until it reaches the base, where it melds with a carved snake head. This tribute to Mayan astronomy is replicated every night in a sound-and-light show.

The entire 1,000-acre site contains many more structures, inscriptions and sculptures which mirror the sophisticated lifestyle of the Mayas – the priests, astronomers, aristocrats, traders, bureaucrats and warriors.

Playing the game

Most intriguing is the Pok-Ta-Pok Ball Court, the size of a football field. Seven other ball courts at Chichén Itzá are much smaller. There was a Royal Box one end, facing a VIP stand at the other. The high side walls produced excellent acoustics, enabling the king to overhear conversation among those who might be plotting at the other end.

Experts have deduced from carved stone panels how the game was played. Two teams of seven struggled to project a ball through a stone ring, high up on each side wall, without using hands, feet or head. The winning captain had the supreme honour of having his head removed, as a gift to the gods. He was thus assured of instant and honoured acceptance into heaven.

Heads you lose

Some experts declare that it was the losing captain who lost his head, but that doesn't make such an interesting story. The gods prefer only the best. To decapitate the loser would have been a second-best offering.

Adjoining the Ball Court is the Wall of Skulls, with carvings that suggest that here was the platform for the decapitation rituals, with eagles and warriors shown eating the human hearts.

Further across the site is the superb Temple of the Warriors with Chac-Mool, the semi-recumbent being with a bowl on his lap, possibly to receive sacrificial human hearts. Chac-Mool today more often appears on tourist posters. Alongside this temple is the Group of the Thousand Columns, probably used as a market place.

These great monuments are part of the northern complex, nearest to the Visitor Centre. Monuments to the south are even older, including a remarkable Observatory which has provided many clues to its precision construction as sightlines for astronomy.

4.3 Uxmal

From Chichén Itzá it takes several hours to reach Uxmal, due south of Mérida along Highway 281. In contrast to the general flatness of the Yucatán, the Uxmal area is somewhat more hilly. The Puuc hills give their name to Uxmal's unique architectural style, identified by thick walls covered by thinner hand-carved slabs of stone to form a mosaic. Development of a local cement also allowed the use of wide arches, huge gateways and impressive rooms.

Pleasing the rain god

Uxmal, meaning three times built or occupied, was the capital of an empire which embraced south eastern Yucatán. The site is a complete mosaic art gallery, with innumerable graphics of birds, animals and Yucatán huts of the same type to be seen today.

Dozens of masks depict Chaac the rain god, who played a major part in religious ceremonies. The Mayas depended on Chaac's goodwill for their maize harvest. Without his full cooperation there would be famine in the land.

Counting the years

A popular legend claims that the Pyramid of the Magician at Uxmal was built in a single day. More likely, each of its five different levels was added possibly at intervals of 52 years – a time-scale which had great religious and astronomical significance. The pyramid temple is decorated with rain-god masks, intricate mosaics and rich latticework.

Past the Magician's Pyramid is the Nunnery Quadrangle – a name given by early Spaniards who thought the layout resembled a Spanish convent. Stone artwork covers the facades with monkeys, birds, snakes, male nudes, thatched huts, turtles and Chaac the Rain-god ad infinitum.

Here is setting for an enthralling sound and light show which brings the details even more vividly to life – in Spanish at 7 p.m., English at 9 p.m.

On the upper level of the site, past a Ball Court, is another Grand Pyramid and the magnificent Palace of the Governor, over a hundred yards long, and dating from early 10th century. Alignment of the doorways is precisely linked to the orbit of planet Venus, using the Altar of the Jaguar as a sightline.

Close by, the House of the Turtles makes an excellent viewpoint for photographs of the Magician's Pyramid rising above the greenery.

4.4 Mérida

In the colonial city of Mérida, capital of the state of Yucatán, only the most important avenues have names. All the other grid-pattern streets are numbered – north-south streets with even numbers; east-west streets with odd numbers.

Otherwise the city feels like southern Spain. Private houses have wrought iron balconies, grills on ground-floor windows, and elegant patios. The central Plaza Major was laid out in 1542, when the *conquistador* Francisco de Montejo built over a former Mayan town.

The original Montejo palace comprised one entire side of the square. The central part of Casa de Montejo continued in the family's ownership until 1970, and has since been acquired for the bank offices of Banamex.

Family tree, set in stone

The highly ornate main entrance is dominated by sculptures that display the Montejo family tree, with lower-level knights standing on the heads of defeated Mayas. Inside, the beautiful patio is a cool green oasis, open during banking hours.

The Renaissance style 16th-century Cathedral, the oldest in Mexico, was built like a fortress, using stones from the Mayan temple which had occupied the site. Inside is a huge cross, among the largest in the world. Especially interesting is a 16th-century painting of Uxmal, which shows how that Mayan site looked when Franciscan priests were busy baptising the natives. The organ, still in use, was installed in 1607.

The Governor's Palace was the official residence of the governor of Yucatán until 1948, when it changed its function. Today it's notable for a dramatic series of murals, created by Fernando Castro Pacheco in 1974.

The paintings illustrate regional history, with an explosive mural above the main staircase, based on the Mayan legend that man was created from a sheaf of corn.

Chamber of horrors

In the historical salon – a magnificent marble-floored room – murals portray gruesome scenes of Mayan history, heavily slanted towards anti-colonialism. There is torture by the Inquisition, the mass burning of Mayan heretics, slavery and ultimate revolution.

A panel chronicles the 17th and 18th century English pirates who attacked the coast and occupied Belize. Another panel depicts the trade in sisal, produced on vast haciendas which made the owners rich enough to build fine mansions in Mérida.

Many of those stately homes are located on Paseo de Montejo, the prime avenue of Mérida, where a monument was erected in 1946 to depict a sculptor's view of Mayan history.

An excellent Anthropological Museum on Montejo Avenue was converted from the Palacio Canton which formerly housed a Mexican general. Open Tue-Sat 8-20 hrs, Sun 8-14 hrs, the museum can offer wider understanding of Mayan achievements.

The night scene

Mérida by night takes on new magic with flood-lighting of the Plaza Major. The 18th-century City Hall with its clock tower looks like a stage set. Restaurants in the colonnade serve Mexican food at very reasonable prices.

In some of the other central squares, open-air cafés and restaurants add music to the romantic setting. On several evenings a week, free concerts are performed in various open-air locations. Performances are given by local folk ballet companies, with the accent on Yucatán costumes and themes. The local audience can be just as enthusiastic as the visitors.

Charming horse carriages feature half-hour tours for a negotiable £4 or £5 – a delightful way of rounding off a memorable evening in this typical Colonial city.

4.5 *Tulum and Cobá*

Eighty miles south of Cancún, or 40 miles from Playa del Carmen, Tulum is the only Mayan city built on the coast. Easily reached along Highway 307, Tulum rates among the area's biggest attractions.

Built in the 10th century, and reaching its peak from the 12th to the 15th centuries, Tulum is probably the only Mayan city still fully inhabited when the first *conquistadors* arrived in 1518.

The Spaniards saw a massive castle-like structure, perched on a 40-ft limestone cliff, and assumed it was a fortress which they called El Castillo. In fact it was a temple, not built with any military intent.

The site overlooks a beautiful sandy bay which served as a harbour for Mayan sailors who traded along the Caribbean coast. Archaeologists have deduced that lanterns in two small windows of El Castillo cast beams to pinpoint the only narrow entrance through an off-shore reef.

Tulum is the only completely walled Mayan settlement known. This surrounding wall was not intended for defence, but just to mark the city boundary. Tulum is much smaller than other much-visited Mayan sites. But because its sixty main buildings are closely grouped, their impact is greater.

The Temple of the Descending God was so named because of the upside-down winged god carved over its entrance. In the Temple of the Frescoes, 13th-century wall paintings depict traditional Mayan deities.

Jungle take-over

From Tulum it's a 25-mile drive to Cobá, along a narrow strip of concrete through the jungle. In occasional clearings attempts have been made to build a house or commercial enterprise, like "Welcome to Cenote Car Wash". But if the project fails, the jungle rapidly closes in, and recaptures its territory.

The Cobá highways

Essentially that is the story of Cobá, which was one of the region's most important Mayan cities from about 550 to 1000 AD. Spread over an area of 27 square miles, the city of 40,000 people and 20,000 structures was the hub for an impressive road system, including a raised causeway more than 30 feet wide.

How this engineering marvel was used is a mystery, since the Mayan had neither wheeled vehicles nor domestic beasts of burden.

Today, this city in the jungle, surrounded by lakes, is the least disturbed and the least explored of all the peninsula's Mayan sites. Although a well-trodden path leads from the site entrance to the main pyramid, visitors need to be vigilant and look carefully.

There are foliage-encrusted mounds between the trees. Each mound is a building which has yet to be uncovered, because rubble, trees and shrubs have taken over.

Hunting for pyramids

Then, round a corner of the trail, you suddenly find the Nohoch Mul temple, a magnificent pyramid 140 feet high. It's like something out of Indiana Jones, and you expect snakes to come gliding out of the steps.

With steady nerve and energy, it's possible to climb to the top, for a great view over the jungle. Hillocks that rise above the treetops are more temples and pyramids that await archaeologists of the future. A mere 5% of Cobá has been cleared.

Meanwhile Cobá is home to magnificent bird life, which you can hear but probably cannot see through the dense foliage. In this jungle terrain, wear trousers rather than shorts, and good shoes or trainers. Action by the rain god makes the paths very muddy.

Chapter Five

The Pacific coast

5.1 Introducing Puerto Vallarta

Acapulco was the first major resort to be built along Mexico's Pacific coast, and now caters for 3 million visitors a year. Today its main Pacific rival is Puerto Vallarta, about 600 miles north. In between there are scattered beach resorts patronised by Mexican families and travellers who prefer to go off-beat.

Until 1964 Puerto Vallarta was little known. Banderas Bay was explored by the Spaniards in the 1550s; and legends say that English and Dutch pirates sometimes relaxed here. Otherwise nothing much happened for 300 years.

In 1851 the first inhabitants settled along the Cuale River – a few farmers, fishermen and miners. The tiny port at the river mouth was called Las Peñas. Salt was transported into the interior to refine silver, which was then shipped out.

By 1918 the sleepy fishing village had grown to 1,500 residents, remote from events beyond the surrounding jungle-covered mountains. In that year Las Peñas was renamed Puerto Vallarta, in honour of Ignacio L. Vallarta, a State governor during the Mexican Revolution and author of the Mexican constitution.

Puerto Vallarta still continued to slumber for another half-century, with modest development as a resort frequented mainly by families from the nearest large city, Guadalajara, 240 miles away. By 1963, the town had 11,000 inhabitants.

The iguana romance

The town's big break came in 1964, when the famed Hollywood director John Huston arrived to film Tennessee William's *Night of the Iguana*. The movie's star, Richard Burton, was joined on location by Elizabeth Taylor, and the couple's torrid love affair made headlines worldwide. Suddenly the drowsing resort became a magnet for jet-set visitors, seeking the magic which had captivated Richard and Liz.

Since that publicity boost, Puerto Vallarta has never looked back. Developers and multinational hotel groups bought land north and south of the village, but left the centre untouched. Condominiums, shopping malls and high-rise hotels began to line the waterfront.

Today, Puerto Vallarta is a bustling and cosmopolitan resort of some 250,000 residents, of whom most are connected with tourism in one way or another, to serve over 1.5 million annual visitors.

Despite Puerto Vallarta's popularity and dynamic growth, the original centre keeps its charm. Cobbled streets are lined with white stucco buildings roofed with red tiles. Wrought iron balconies overflow with bougainvillaea. Visitors enjoy all the rich warmth and colour of Old Mexico, and are greeted everywhere with smiles and friendly *holas*.

Closely backed by jungle-clad foothills of the rugged Sierra Madre mountains, the countryside is only a few city blocks away. When nightlife ends, roosters start crowing to welcome the dawn.

Private and group horseback rides are available from Rancho El Charro into the lush coastal hills. Guided coach tours offer half-day trips through farming villages and into the jungle.

The principal hotels are spaced along the miles of gorgeous beach, with very frequent and low-cost bus services (about 20p any distance) to and from downtown. Further round the Bahia de Las

Banderas – Mexico's largest natural bay – is Nuevo Vallarta, an enclave of mainly all-inclusive resorts and villas located north of the airport.

The huge Banderas Bay runs from Punta Mita in the State of Nayarit in the north to Cabo Corrientes in Jalisco to the south. The curved coastline offers 25 miles of golden beaches, too numerous to list.

The liveliest beach is close to River Cuale in the centre of Puerto Vallarta. Named Playa de los Muertos from its pirate days, it has officially been renamed Playa del Sol – roughly translating from Dead Men's Beach to Sunshine Beach. But the historic name sounds much more exciting.

The most tranquil beaches are along the north shore en route to Punta Mita. Some of the prettiest coves and inlets can be reached only by sea. Numerous boat trips combine fishing, lunch, open bar, sunbathing and snorkelling in a full day of activity or relaxation.

Puerto Vallarta is the seaside resort of the State of Jalisco, of which Guadalajara is the capital. Jalisco prides itself on being the source of everything that is 'real' Mexico: of mariachi music and all the *charro* traditions of cowboys, sombreros, Mexican-style rodeos called *charreadas*, superb horsemanship, and hearty eating of hominy stew, beans and chillies. If you want a taster of these pleasures, Puerto Vallarta can provide.

5.2 Arrival and orientation

The Gustavo Diaz Ordaz International Airport is located four miles north of Puerto Vallarta, and is very handy for charter flights from Europe. Direct scheduled services are available from major cities of USA and Canada, or with connecting flights by Aéromexico or Mexicana via Mexico City or Guadalajara.

Typical of most Mexican airports, the newly remodelled terminal has polished marble floors, plenty of souvenir shopping for finishing up pesos before departure, exchange desks which give very poor rates, and a restaurant and bar.

Fixed-price transport
For independent travellers there are frequent taxi or minibus transfers from the airport at reasonable set tariffs. There's no need to haggle. Just pay at the taxi desk, and they'll assign transport.

A modern four-lane highway serves all the main hotels, and the journey south takes only a few minutes. For Nuevo Vallarta the journey is equally swift, with the new resort just a brief journey north.

Nuevo Vallarta is located across the River Ameca, which marks the boundary between the State of Jalisco and the State of Nayarit. These two States are in different time zones. Mountain Standard Time for Nayarit is one hour later than Central Standard Time. In practice, Nuevo Vallarta hotels follow the same hours as in Puerto Vallarta, to avoid the risk of misunderstandings and missed flights.

Several times an hour, low-cost public buses connect Nuevo Vallarta hotels with downtown Puerto Vallarta. In Puerto Vallarta itself, bus stops every few hundred yards make it extremely easy and cheap to get around.

If you prefer a taxi, ask a bell-boy the fare, which is set by zones. A pound or two covers most town destinations, but sometimes cabbies try to charge a bit more.

5.3 Exploring Puerto Vallarta
Take a ride into the downtown area, called El Pueblo. Along the main highway is the Villa Vallarta shopping mall, the biggest in Puerto Vallarta, where just about everything is available. Then comes the **Malecón**, a delightful waterfront promenade lined with colourful shops and restaurants. Bars invite you for a Happy Hour, two drinks for the price of one.

Seafront promenade

Into this area and side streets are packed many more restaurants, nightclubs and discos. Art exhibits are often displayed along the walkway. Several attractive sculptures are a popular subject for shutterbugs, including a giant bronze sea horse and a group of frisky dolphins.

The Malecón is built rather high above the road level, to avoid flooding when rain cascades down the steep cobbled side streets. These residential roads, like rough ski slopes, are lined with many charming and beautiful houses. Cobbles are retained to help conserve the old-world charm. It's a city regulation that even the more modern streets are cobbled, to calm the traffic.

Town centre

The old town is focussed around **Plaza Mayor**, overlooked by the principal church and City Hall, where a helpful tourist information office is located. Every Sunday evening, from 6 till 8 pm, Mexican music is played in the bandstand – a free performance for locals and visitors alike.

The Church of Guadalupe is El Pueblo's most visible landmark, built mainly between 1918 and 1951 and theoretically still not finished. The steeple is topped by a concrete replica of the crown worn by Carlota, empress of Mexico in the 1860s. It has become Puerto Vallarta's symbol, endlessly repeated in brochures and in the tourist art sold on the nearby waterfront.

All around, dozens of boutiques, craft shops and fine art galleries offer full scope for shoppers. A municipal market handles more basic products, with bargaining potential for traditional giftware.

Beneath a bridge over the River Cuale is a narrow island, which is a green haven for shops and restaurants. Most shops are open 10-21 hrs, but they close for siesta. Typical local products include hand-made leather sandals, blown glass lamps, and wood carvings.

Jet-set gringos

Just across the bridge is Old Vallarta, with even more rough-and-ready cobblestones. A little further up-river is so-called **Gringo Gulch**, settled by the first wave of expatriates who converted the area into a little America. Elizabeth Taylor bought a hillside white house called Casa Kimberly in 1965, after the movie *Night of the Iguana* was completed.

Later, after a second divorce from Elizabeth Taylor, Richard Burton also bought a house, two blocks away, when he married a new wife named Susan Hunt. The thatched-roof house is called Casa Bursan, a combination of Burton and Susan.

5.4 All the sports

Puerto Vallarta's year-round sunshine, beaches and tropical mountains are heaven for those who prefer· active vacations. Every imaginable watersport is available along the 25-mile shoreline. From most hotel beaches there are facilities for water-skiing, windsurfing, deep sea fishing, sailing, scuba diving, snorkelling, catamaran and yacht excursions and parasailing. At all-inclusive hotels, such as those at Nuevo Vallarta, watersports are mostly free except when engine power is used.

Compared with the flat Caribbean coast with its offshore coral reefs, the mountainous Pacific coast offers less potential for underwater action. Likewise the waters, churned by silt-laden runoff from the mountains, do not have the same sparkling clarity of the Caribbean. For scuba-diving and snorkelling, Los Arcos has been designated as an underwater national park, with choice of deep and shallow dives.

More expert divers can also experience some of the rich deep-sea life of the bay, home to dolphins and sea turtles, giant mantas and migrating whales. The bay is a regular breeding ground for humpback whales, who arrive between late December and mid-March.

Turtle watch

Totally protected turtles lay eggs on the beaches during summer. These nesting sites are fenced around with netting during the 45 days to hatch. Besides being a memorable feature of the underwater scenery, sea turtles feed on jellyfish, keeping them in check.

For deep-sea fishermen, November to May is the best season for sailfish and marlin. Smaller game such as wahoo and yellowtail are caught year-round.

On land, golf, tennis and horseback riding are among the most popular sports. Spectators can watch something they never see at home – donkey polo. For golfers, Puerto Vallarta offers two challenging courses: Los Flamingos with jungle-lined fairways; and Marina Vallarta Country Club with scenic lakes, ponds and lagoons.

Horse riders can choose trails around the city or in the mountains, or sign up for escorted tours through rural villages and spectacular scenery.

5.5 *Land and sea excursions*

It's worth exploring what else the Puerto Vallarta region can offer besides those gorgeous beaches. Here are some options.

Serving as an introduction is a 5-hour **Tropical Tour** which visits a charming small town, El Pitillal, which looks like Puerto Vallarta of 30 years ago. The main square has the standard Mexican layout with the essential public buildings around each side: church, city hall and jail. Street vendors operate taco stalls, or offer sugarcane juice, newly pressed through a mangle.

The tour then returns for a complete briefing on Puerto Vallarta before driving south along the coast to Mismaloya Beach, where the Iguana movie was set. Up into the jungle hills, a dreamy location overlooks a river. Great boulders are washed by pools and waterfalls. Local kids dive brilliantly for coins. Several restaurants include the word Eden or Paradise in their names.

Jungle Tour

Another popular half-day circuit goes north to fruit and vegetable plantations and then turns off into the hills and jungle. Stops are made at tiny villages for a close-up of peasant life, including a home visit to see how tortillas are made. Cash income derives from mango trees, coconuts, avocados, water melons, guavas, pineapples and bananas; tomato and cucumber.

Walking along a woodland path, the guide holds forth on the plants, trees and secretive wildlife. Pumas or jaguars are unlikely, but maybe you'll see an iguana or a big spider. The interest lies in the jungle ecology, brought to life by a well-informed tour leader.

Longer trips

More ambitious is a two-day tour to Guadalajara, 187 road miles by air-conditioned coach through unspoilt scenery. A typical itinerary with early-morning start gives a full afternoon of city sightseeing; overnight at a central hotel; Tlaquepaque next morning and a halt at a tequila distillery on the homeward journey. (See Chapter 7).

Three-day options feature Mexico City, or even longer to include other colonial cities. Varied itineraries combine flights by Mexicana or Aeroméxico, with coach travel. (See Chapters 6 and 7).

By boat

Numerous boat trips are on offer – to varied beaches for swimming and snorkelling; by day, at sunset or at night. Some idyllic beaches can be reached only by sea, with no road access. But they mostly have a beach restaurant where the food is simple but good; and plenty of cool drinks.

A typical **Sunset Cruise** includes music, dance and open bar during a journey along the coast, past Los Arcos – rock arches eroded by the waves to form hollows and caverns, rich in bird life. Many day trips stop here for snorkelling. As the sun sets, pelicans and other birds come gliding in to their favourite perch for the night. The scene hasn't changed for the past few thousand years.

5.6 *Nightlife*

When it comes to dining, dancing and late night romancing, Puerto Vallarta does it con gusto. Start the evening with a bar-hopping swing, with a sunset margarita at a quiet hilltop terrace or piña colada at a boisterous gringo bar. To set the mood, most bars feature Happy Hour drinks, two for the price of one.

Dozens of restaurants in town and at the resort hotels serve a full range of international cuisine. Choice goes from open-air beach restaurants to elegant establishments that feature gourmet cuisine and candlelight. Live rock and jazz are offered at over a dozen high-activity pubs and discos in El Centro and south of the Rio Cuale. As midnight approaches, nightclubs are in full swing.

In several locations, Mexican Fiesta shows give you a set-price buffet meal, open bar, folklore music and dancing, with Mariachi musicians and other performers.

Entertainment at all-inclusive hotels is provided every night, with a full Mexican show at least once a week. The main after-dinner shows are usually followed by music in the piano bar, and a disco somewhere else in the complex.

Chapter Six

Mexico City break

6.1 Capital highlights

Mexico City rates as the world's most populated city, 19 million at last count. The aircraft landing is dramatic, into a wide valley, 7,220 feet high, surrounded by volcanic peaks that rise to over 17,000 feet, with deeply fissured foothills.

When Cortéz and his Spaniards arrived over a mountain pass in 1519, they discovered the astonishing culture of the Aztecs. At this supreme height of Aztec power, the city was already the largest in the New World, probably with 400,000 population. Cortés described it as being even more beautiful than Granada.

Curiously the wandering Aztecs were relative newcomers, having made it the capital of their empire only from around AD 1325. They called their city Tenochtitlán, based on a large island in the middle of Lake Texcoco which once covered the entire valley. The city's ceremonial centre of great temple-topped white pyramids, palaces, gardens and wide avenues, were all connected to lakeshore satellite towns by a well-engineered network of canals and roads.

As the population grew, the Aztecs built islands by filling huge wicker rafts with soil. Eventually most of the surrounding waters were drained, to form the land mass where Mexico City now sprawls. Xochimilco, south of the city, still depends on the floating gardens from ancient times.

New World, new city

Within two years of marvelling at this magical city, the Spaniards were triumphant conquerors. They promptly began tearing down the Aztec monuments and replacing them with churches, palaces and other public buildings needed for their New World capital.

The Spanish city plan of the 1520's followed the original layout of the Aztec ceremonial centre, with highways that followed the line of historic canals linked to the surrounding lake. The soil was watery and porous. Since then, many of the heavier colonial-age stone buildings have tilted and partially sunk into the loam, with ground floors now operating as basements.

Visitors today can span the centuries. Among the sightseeing highlights are the surviving Aztec remains (mostly in museums), the great 16th-century monuments built by the *conquistadors*, the colonial buildings of later centuries, the boulevards of the 19th century and the vibrant new architecture of the 20th.

Gardeners to the Aztecs

Away from the centre, the market gardeners of Xochimilco can claim direct descent from their Indian ancestors who supplied the Aztecs with fruit, flowers and vegetables. Only 37 miles from Mexico City's centre are the pyramids of Teotihuacán, a thriving city 2,000 years ago but already overgrown and forgotten long before the Aztecs arrived.

Mexico City is known today for its snarled-up traffic and heavy pollution. But at least the daytime temperatures are ideal for sightseeing, about 70 degrees maximum with cooler evenings.

Miniscule taxis are metered and cheap, while the Metro system is efficient and costs peanuts any distance. During construction of the subway system, many Aztec ruins were discovered and are being carefully preserved. Superb museums bring that ancient world vividly to life.

Into the 21st century

Meanwhile the present-day citizens of Mexico City are not living in the past, and even the traditional siesta no longer operates. The city offers a wealth of cultural activities, modern art, excellent restaurants and exuberant nightlife. It would all take weeks to explore. On a brief visit, the best option is to sample the riches by concentrating on a few selected areas.

6.2 The historic centre

The heart of Mexico City is the **Zócalo**, the world's second largest square after Moscow's Red Square. Here was the original site of Aztec ceremonies. Dominating the Zócalo is the enormous **Cathedral** – the largest in Latin America – which took almost three centuries to build. It combines Spanish Renaissance architecture and early 19th-century French neoclassical style.

Inside the Cathedral, the Altar of the Kings and the Altar of Forgiveness were built and carved by Jeronimo de Balbas in the decade around 1725, and contain paintings surrounded by golden columns, sculptures, mouldings, angels and other Baroque decorations.

The **Sagrario** which is sinking alongside is the Cathedral's sacristy, built in the 18th century. In the northwest corner of the Zócalo is the National Pawn Shop on the site of an Aztec palace, where Cortés stayed as an honoured guest in 1519, and where Móctezuma II was killed a year or two later.

The northeast corner is occupied by the open-air remains of the **Templo Mayor** (Main Temple) of the Aztecs. Hundreds of sculptures and artifacts were excavated here in 1978 and 1981 and are displayed in the adjacent Templo Mayor Museum, converted from a colonial mansion. The prime exhibit is a replica of the eight-ton stone disc representing Coyolxauhqui, Goddess of the Moon. The original is housed in the Museum of Anthropology.

The Diego Rivera murals

The **National Palace**, occupying the entire east side of the Zócalo, was built by Cortés on the site of Móctezuma's palace. Over the centuries it has served as official residence of viceroys and presidents, and now houses government offices.

Enter the palace to see the world's most stunning murals, painted by Diego Rivera from 1929 to 1952. They depict the entire history of Mexico, from pre-Columbian days to the present century. Enormous murals up the main staircase are crammed with drama, reflecting the artist's view of class struggle through the ages.

Around the first floor are visions of daily life in pre-Conquest times. The Aztec capital is vividly portrayed in the mural *La Gran Tenochtitlán*. Incidentally, this first-floor gallery overlooks the main patio, in which Cortés staged the continent's first bullfight in 1529.

City Hall, rebuilt in 1720, lies on the south side of the Zócalo, while almost the entire length of the Merchants Arcade on the west side, dating from 17th century, is taken by jeweller shops.

At weekends a corner of the Zócalo becomes an open-air market, lively with local families enjoying a stroll. Indian musicians and folk-dancers perform. Women sell corn on the cob, cooked over a brazier, and served with added salt and a twist of lime juice.

Other stalls offer *sincronizadas*, which are heated tortillas with ham and cheese. There are sweaters and shoes for sale, children's toys and musical instruments, nut products, costume dolls, tapes and compact discs.

Heading west from the Zócalo, it's just a short taxi ride or a 20-minute walk along Avenido Madero to the downtown business district.

En route are several buildings of interest, including the 18th-century baroque **Iturbide Palace** and the **Temple of San Francisco** which was the 16th-century HQ of the Franciscan order, but sinking.

Business district

The ornate **House of Tiles** (Casa de los Azulejos) is a 16th-century mansion totally sheathed in blue and white glazed tiles. It is now a restaurant and book shop. Further along is the 44-storey **Torre Latinoamericana**, Mexico's third-highest skyscraper; and, close by, the monumental **Central Post Office**.

If you enjoyed the Rivera murals in the National Palace, make time for the **Palace of Fine Arts** (Palacio de Bellas Artes). This sumptuous building of Italian marble took 30 years to build and is the home of the world-famous Ballet Folklórico, and also National Symphony Orchestra.

The theatre's stained glass curtain of volcanoes outside Mexico City was designed by Tiffany of New York. Upstairs is the world's best collection of Mexican mural art. Open Tue-Sun 10-18 hrs. Check on performances of the folklore ballet.

6.3 Reforma/Chapultepec Park

The elegant Paseo de la Reforma crosses Mexico City from west to northeast. This grand 7½-mile boulevard was built in 1862 by Emperor Maximilian, who was inspired by the Champs Elysées in Paris. The highway linked Maximilian's residence at Chapultepec Castle with downtown.

Today, sleek office buildings, leading banks and the Stock Exchange line the boulevard. Warned by the sinking of so many heavy stone buildings over the years, today's architects base construction techniques on a lighter steel frame, with wall coverings of plastic and glass.

Major roundabouts along Reforma are marked by bronze statues and monuments. There's a memorial to Christopher Columbus, who seems to be waving for a taxi. Along the roadside numerous statues honour eminent doctors, lawyers, generals and politicians. Then comes a tribute to Cuauhtémoc, the last of the Aztec kings. The Independence Monument, El Angel, marks a corner of the Zona Rosa (see details below).

Chapultepec Park

At the western end of Paseo de la Reforma is Chapultepec Park, covering some 1,700 acres. Los Piños, the official home of Mexico's President, is located in the park, while Chapultepec Castle houses the National Museum of History.

Especially at weekends the public areas of the Park are filled with family picnickers, attracted by the Zoo, an amusement park, and a lake with rowing boats. There's also free entrance on Sundays to the world-class museums which are spread around the Park. Like elsewhere, the museums are closed on Mondays, but with minimal entrance fees on other weekdays.

The choice in Chapultepec Park includes the Museum of Natural History, The Museum of Modern Art, and the Museo del Caracol, which features historic dioramas and the 1917 constitution. The Rufino Tamayo Museum displays Tamayo's avant-garde murals and his international collection of over 160 other modern artists, including Picasso, Dalí and Francis Bacon.

Top choice museum

If you can visit only one museum, the prime choice should be the National Museum of Anthropology, considered one of the world's finest, with stunning architecture and layout. The galleries display thousands of artifacts and exhibits from Mexico's 3,000 years of human evolution. The archaeological treasures are breathtaking, and give a complete overview of the rich cultures from long-past centuries.

Equally interesting is the museum's upper floor, which portrays the life and customs of indigenous groups of today.

If time is brief, just pick the galleries which cover the areas you plan to visit during your holiday: the Maya room for the Yucatán; or the Teotihuacán room for better understanding of the Pyramids outside Mexico City. The Hall of the Mexicas covers the Aztec period.

Birdmen of the Aztecs

Occasional performances are given of ancient music, using authentic instruments. Another attraction in the grounds is a *volador* – a very tall maypole from which four performers launch themselves on ropes from the top. Head down, they circle 13 times, lower and lower, until they land gently as birds. It's another Aztec ritual.

Further up the Paseo de la Reforma leads to the residential area of Polanco: the city's wealthiest district, with luxury homes, fine restaurants and shopping that rival the Zona Rosa.

6.4 Zona Rosa

The Pink Zone – the Zona Rosa – is an up-market district with boutiques, hotels, tea-rooms, restaurants, discos and nightclubs. Located south of Reforma, about halfway between the Zócalo and Chapultepec Park, the Zona Rosa has a distinctly European feel, with pavement cafés.

Most of the streets are named after European place-names. Walking up parallel grid streets such as Calle Denmark, Naples, Nice, Genoa, Florence, Warsaw, Prague, Seville or Toledo, you'll cross Liverpool Street and London Street.

The landmark for the Zona Rosa is the Independence Monument known as El Angel, a slender column with an eight-ton golden angel perched on top to represent the Goddess of Liberty. Erected in 1910 to mark the centenary of Mexican Independence from Spanish rule, the monument is regarded as an emblem of Mexico City. Peace, Work, Justice and Government are represented by the statues at the bottom.

Mexico City is one big dining room, with food stalls on every street corner, and thousands of restaurants of every grade and cuisine. You can sample the full range in the Zona Rosa, with guitar music as you eat. Otherwise, for the full mariachi treatment, take a cab to Plaza de Garibaldi, where bands wait to be hired. Numerous restaurants and nightspots surround the action.

6.5 *Where to go on Sunday*

Plan your sightseeing trips with Sunday in mind. Shops are closed, and roads are less jammed with traffic. All museums are open, but are closed on Monday.

For inveterate shoppers, varied antiques and junk items are on sale at the Sundays-only Lagunilla Market where local artisans display their art and craft products. This flea market is located north along Paseo de la Reforma, turning onto Calle Rayon at the monument to San Martín, the liberator of Argentina.

Sculpture, paintings and engravings are displayed Sunday afternoons at an open-air art show in Sullivan Park, very close to the Zona Rosa. A visit can be combined with time at the Museum of Anthropology (which stays open till 19 hrs on Sunday), and to savour the weekend jollity of Chapultepec Park.

On Sundays, too, regular Mexican folk-dance performances are given either at the Museum of Anthropology, or at the Palace of Fine Arts. Check details, to make a reservation.

Sunday is also the best possible day to see the floating gardens of Xochimilco with a boat ride on the network of canals. Located 22 miles out on the southeastern outskirts of Mexico City, Xochimilco specialises in a daily flower market, run by the local Indians whose ancestors have worked the island nurseries and market gardens since Aztec times.

Sunday is the peak day for Mexican family parties who flock out from the city to buy flowers, take pleasure boat rides and enjoy floating picnics.

For starters, imagine an approach road that's like a mile-long garden centre, glowing with tropical plants. Near the car park, dozens of restaurants and barbecues offer take-away pork, turkey, rabbit and chicken. In fierce competition, chefs wave tasty morsels to passers-by, trumpeting the quality and price.

Gondola serenade

By the canalside, colourful flat-bottom boats await, each painted with a girl's name in flowery designs. Every boat has a table and benches. The boats are called gondolas, but are shaped like very wide canopied punts. Hire charges are modest, based on size, with your boatman punting along canals that wend past the cultivated islands.

If picnic supplies run out, floating vendors cook tacos or corn-on-the-cobs to order, or sell soft drinks, beer or toffee apples. Gliding along are mariachi groups, who play and sing favourite tunes at 20 or 30 pesos per melody.

Boats were originally used in pre-colonial times to transport produce into the Aztec city. During this century, the boats have been used for Sunday trips. It's a charming view of real Mexico, seeing how the locals enjoy a day out.

University City

The route to or from Xochemilco can include a visit to the University campus, with sight of ambitious sport facilities built for the 1968 Olympics, including the 110,000-seat Aztec Stadium.

Mexico has a long history of higher education, with its first university dating from 1553. By the early 20th century, colleges and universities were scattered haphazard across the city.

Funding for a completely new complex came from taking over foreign-owned oil companies. Building began in 1952 and broke all world records for academic construction, with an entire university built in only six years. At the inauguration, capacity was 38,000 students. Since then, the numbers have increased to the present level of 325,000, besides those at technical schools.

The campus covers five square miles of a former volcanic moonscape, landscaped and well wooded. Much of the ultra-modern architecture is stunning, embellished with monumental mosaics, murals and sculptures. The Library, covered in mosaics by Juan O'Gorman, is outstanding.

6.6 To the Pyramids

Mexico City is ideally placed for reaching historic sites and cities on day-trip or overnight excursions. Depending on time available, a short-list could include the Pyramids of Teotihuacán; Tula and Tepotzotlán; Cuernavaca and Taxco; Puebla and Tlaxcala.

With half a day to spare, the Pyramids of Teotihuacán easily rank as the prime choice, 37 miles northeast of central Mexico City. This pilgrimage site flourished from about 300 or 500 BC to 700 AD. At its peak, the city covered a larger area than imperial Rome. Its prosperity came from local volcanic quarries of obsidian, used for making knives, arrowheads, tools and weapons.

Although much is unknown, there are signs that its people came from the east, worshipped the rain god and used human sacrifice in their ceremonies. When the Aztecs came to the region, the city had long been abandoned.

Two great monuments dominate the flat landscape. The Pyramids of the Sun and Moon are surrounded by wide plazas and esplanades, lined with platforms and structures.

The Sun Pyramid stands 216 feet high and is 240 yards square at the base – similar ground measurements to the Cheops pyramid in Egypt, but only half the height. Topping the pyramid was a temple and an astronomical observatory.

At the site's main entrance, the Temple of Quetzalcóatl is filled with sculptural decoration showing the plumed serpent in motion. There are numerous masks of Quetzalcóatl and of Tlaloc, the God of Water and Rain. The Street of the Dead is very broad, two miles long, linking this temple with the two pyramids. En route there are housing complexes, more temples and palaces.

The overall impact is breathtaking, even if you don't go panting to the top of the pyramids. The site museum contains sculptures of sacred animals such as jaguars, eagles, serpents and frogs.

Basilica of Guadalupe

The route to and from Teotihuacán passes by the Plaza of Three Cultures – a site which includes the remains of an Aztec pyramid, an early Franciscan convent building, and 20th-century apartments.

Further along is the Basilica of Guadalupe, the holiest catholic shrine in Latin America. A vision of the Virgin of Guadalupe in December 1531 drew Christian pilgrims to the site where an Aztec temple had formerly been dedicated to the earth mother. Recognised by the Pope in 1754, the Virgin of Guadalupe became the patron saint of Mexico, and today is the patron saint of another twelve nations of the Americas.

A 17th-century basilica has been sinking unsteadily, and cannot be entered. An ultra-modern circular replacement, with capacity for over 10,000 worshippers, was designed in 1971 by the avant-garde architect of the National Museum of Anthropology.

Services are held hourly through the day, beginning at 5 a.m. Even to non-Catholics, the experience is deeply touching. Every flower-laden pilgrim wants to see the miracle-working image of Our Lady of Guadalupe. To prevent devotees from clogging up the passage, a moving walkway has been installed. The Virgin's feast day of December 12 is a national holiday.

Chapter Seven

Colonial circle

7.1 Mexico's heartland

The central plateau of Mexico offers a journey into landscape and history. Travellers can enjoy the natural and manmade treasures of the Colonial circle, roughly defined as the area between Mexico City and Guadalajara.

The elevation, between 6,000 and 7,000 feet, ensures springlike conditions during much of the year. The annual average temperature is 65 degrees, though evenings can be chilly in winter.

Even for those who are not geared to Mexican economic and political history, visitors respond to the Colonial legacy. Silver and copper mines brought great wealth to the realm, funding baroque churches, opulent public buildings, mansions and estates.

Several city centres have been designated national historic sites, to preserve their unique architecture, glowing colours and narrow cobblestone streets.

In this region, resistance to Spanish rule found voice and finally triumphed during the early 19th century. The struggle between Spain and the communities scattered among the Sierra Madre mountains left a heritage that defines modern Mexico.

Monuments to the national heroes of independence stand within sight of tributes to Spanish rulers. To walk these historic streets is to retrace the steps in the growth of a nation.

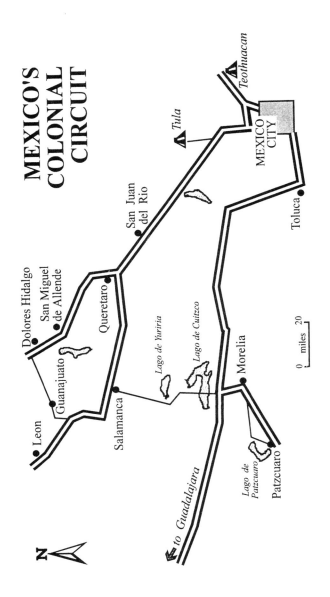

MEXICO'S COLONIAL CIRCUIT

60

Traditional crafts

While the Colonial cities offer delight for history, culture and architecture buffs, they also provide good hunting for shoppers. Each city has a thriving craft tradition, and serves as a market centre for surrounding villages.

In the Pátzcuaro area, for example, markets overflow with high-quality guitars from Paracho, copperware from Santa Clara del Cobre and dolls' house furniture from Quiroga.

San Miguel de Allende is best known for its elaborate tinware, but also displays local wool rugs and blankets, silver jewellery and a stunning range of pottery.

Travelling around the area is easy and convenient. Good motor roads open onto spectacular vistas of rugged mountains. Guided tours range from four days to several weeks, covering every interest.

With fifty designated Colonial cities to explore throughout Mexico, visitors can spend months without running out of new discoveries. Following is a small sample of the key cities which can be linked along the Independence Trail of 1810, through the heart of Mexico.

7.2 The silver cities

Starting out from Mexico City, along the motorway running northwest, a detour is possible to visit **Tula**, capital of the Toltecs from around 950 to 1250 AD. The Toltecs were warriors, but also famed for their wisdom, making advances in writing, architecture, music, medicine, astronomy and agriculture: skills which passed along to the Mayas and the Aztecs.

Tula's principal monument is the Temple of the Morning Star, topped by four colossal warrior statues called *Atlantes*, in full battledress. Behind the pyramid is an elaborately sculpted *Coatepantli*, a wall of serpents; in the central area, two *Chacmool* reclining sculptures, awaiting their tribute of warm human hearts.

Querétaro is a bastion of Colonial art – in the streets, churches, government buildings and squares.

There are many reminders of the city's religious and historical legacy. It was here that plans for Mexican independence were made in 1810, and where the emperor Maximilian was shot 57 years later.

A stroll through the pedestrianized centre can include the cloisters of the regional museum, which is housed in a baroque monastery built in 1731. The tiny Plaza de la Independencia is a Spanish jewel.

The route continues across a plateau of about 6,500 feet, with few crops, but more like a multi-coloured desert with cactus.

San Miguel de Allende is named after the second-in-command of the Independence army of 1810. Declared a National Monument by the Mexican Institute of History and Anthropology, the town was founded in 1542 by the Spaniards, and still retains much of its Colonial charm.

Today, cafés, art galleries and shops line cobblestone streets in the city centre. San Miguel de Allende is an artists' and writers' colony and a retirement home for many North American and European residents. Towering over the central square is a 17th century gothic church.

Dolores Hidalgo was the starting point of Mexico's march to independence from Spanish rule. On 16 September 1810, a parish priest named Father Miguel Hidalgo made the 'shout for independence' which echoed across the nation and launched the Mexican Revolution. The town was later named in Hidalgo's honour.

From here the Independence Trail continued as a somewhat unruly mob, armed with pitchforks and scythes, marched on to San Miguel de Allende, Querétaro, Guanajuato and Morelia. But their violence turned many sympathisers against them.

Guanajuato clings dramatically to a mountainous ravine, the gateway to the region's silver mines. The city's special character is formed by history and geography. As the richest of the colonial silver towns, it built a dazzling display of Baroque theatres, public buildings, mansions and churches. The first battle in the fight for independence took place in Guanajuato, and numerous monuments reflect the city's pride in that event.

Guanajuato is a maze of streets and alleys that wind around hillsides, opening into vistas of brightly painted houses and beautiful small plazas. These passageways are largely traffic-free, since the city's main highways run underground along old mine tunnels and a former riverbed.

The odd layout, and the cobblestone streets, plazas and flower gardens, all give Guanajuato its romantic charm, enhanced by night. The legendary Callejón del Beso is a narrow alley where lovers in opposite houses could lean across from their balconies and enjoy a forbidden kiss.

Guanajuato is made for walking. Every tiny side street seems to lead to pocket gardens, quaint houses or impressive old buildings and monuments. Among the highlights are the Jardín Unión, an elegant plaza ringed with outdoor cafés and a green-coloured theatre; Alhóndiga de Granaditas, a granary that became a fortress during the Independence movement, and is now a historical museum; and the Diego Rivera Museum, birthplace of the famed muralist, now filled with a collection of his paintings.

Lakeland

From Guanajuato the road goes south towards Morelia. The area around Valle de Santiago is highly cultivated, with irrigated plantations of strawberries, asparagus and mixed vegetables. Then come two beautiful lakes – Laguna de Yuriría and Laguna Cuitzéo – as a foretaste of the scenic highlights of Lake Pátzcuaro, ringed by volcanic mountains.

Pátzcuaro, southwest of Morelia, is populated mainly by Tarascan Indians. Whitewashed, tile-roofed houses surround Colonial churches and monasteries that date from the 16th century. The original San Nicolás College building, built in 1540, is now a museum displaying local crafts such as intricate masks, lacquerware, ceramic dishes and hand-woven textiles.

Another recycled building, the House of the Eleven Patios, is an 18th-century Dominican convent that now houses craft workshops with a wide selection of products.

On the idyllic mountain lake, fishermen demonstrate their traditional butterfly-shaped nets. Janitzio Island, in the middle of the lake, is marked by an enormous sculpture of Father Morelos, the local hero of Independence.

Morelia overlooks the valley of Guayangareo and is encircled by spectacular scenery: pine forests, waterfalls, steep mountainsides and small villages. Morelia's historic importance is reflected in its name, which was changed in 1828 from Valladolid to Morelia in honour of its son and revolutionary leader, Father Morelos.

The priest continued the fight for independence after the deaths of Hidalgo and Allende. The house in which Morelos was born is now a museum and cultural centre.

The city's romantic plaza, lovely Colonial buildings, exhilarating climate and wide boulevards make it the aristocrat among Colonial cities, designated by UNESCO as a World Heritage Site. The Baroque-style cathedral overlooking the central square is one of Mexico's tallest churches. Opposite is the state capitol, Palacio de Gobierno, with dramatic murals of Mexican history, painted by the locally-born artist, Alfredo Zalce.

The College of San Nicolás·is the oldest surviving college in the New World, founded in 1540 but moved to this site in 1580.

Culture and crafts

The Museo Michoacáno, an impressive 18th-Century palace, houses pre-Columbian artifacts, Colonial furnishings and other historical items, with staircase murals by Zalce. The 17th-century Clavijero Palace, originally a Jesuit college, is worth visiting for its splendid patio. Another delightful building is the House of Culture in a former convent founded in the 16th century.

Morelia is the main sales outlet for crafts produced by neighbouring Tarascan Indian communities. A good place for shoppers to start is the Casa de las Artesanías in the former Convent of San Francisco.

7.3 Guadalajara

Mexico's second-largest city, population four million, makes a memorable side trip for anyone on holiday in Puerto Vallarta. A two-day swing to Guadalajara is packed with interest, thanks to a city centre which has kept its Colonial charm while becoming a major commercial and business centre. On a circular tour of the Colonial cities, Guadalajara completes the picture of Mexico today, rich in tradition and culture.

Following the usual layout of Mexican towns, sightseeing focusses around the Cathedral - founded in 1542, but taking several centuries to complete, with mismatch of many different styles. The cathedral is surrounded by four plazas, in which the pedestrian is king. The ground plan is like the four elements of a cross, with the cathedral in the centre.

Most walking tours start in the Plaza de Armas, where the Art Nouveau bandstand – a gift from France – was made at the same iron works which produced the Tour Eiffel. The Government Palace across the square is very important in Mexican history. Here, in December 1810, the leader of Mexican Independence, Don Miguel Hidalgo, signed the decree which abolished slavery – fifty years earlier than in USA.

Funded by drink

Building of the Palace started in 1643, but completion was slow. Finally taxes on tequila helped finish the job a century later. The palace has a beautiful patio with orange trees planted in formal style. Staircase murals by José Clemente Orozco commemorate Hidalgo the Liberator.

Another side of the Cathedral faces the Plaza de los Laureles, now renamed Plaza Guadalajara. The City Hall is 20th century, but the design blends well with its surroundings of the Historic Centre. Murals on the main stairway depict the founding of the city. The neighbouring Rotonda de los Hombres Ilustres honours men of science, the arts and public adminstration.

Liberation Square, behind the Cathedral, features a powerful statue of Hidalgo, breaking the chains of slavery. There's an excellent Regional Museum on the north side of the Plaza, with a comprehensive pre-Hispanic collection on the ground floor, colonial art-work upstairs. Open daily except Mon, 9-14 hrs.

Other buildings on the Plaza are the Chamber of Deputies and the Court House. The Degollada Theatre at the far end faces the Cathedral and the ceremonial Mexican flag in the centre. The 19th-century theatre is a replica of La Scala in Milan. The university's prestigious Folkloric Ballet plays here every Sunday morning, with amateur singers and dancers who perform to a highly professional standard. The group makes occasional international journeys, acting as an unofficial ambassador for Mexican culture and tradition. They have performed at the Olympic Games, at World Cup meetings and at the 1992 Expo in Seville.

Foundation Square (Plaza de los Fundadores) is located just behind the Theatre, with a bronze sculpture that depicts the first settlers of Guadalajara in 1542. This square leads into the Plaza Tapatía, which forms a nine-block promenade inaugurated in 1982, with fountains, shady trees and modern sculptures.

Devil's Corner

The State Government Tourist Office is located in the former home of the Spanish Inquisition. As a reminder of that link with the past, a passage alongside, filled with Indian handicraft stalls, is officially named as The Devil's Corner – Pasaje Rincón del Diablo.

The central fountain of Plaza Tapatía features a most unusual sculpture that represents Quetzelcóatl, the plumed serpent. The Plaza finally ends at the Cabañas Cultural Institute which ranks as Mexico's largest colonial building, with 23 patios, designed in 1805-1810 in neo-classical style.

Originally the building was a charitable institution, and became an orphanage for 2,000 children. In 1979 the premises were converted to a cultural purpose with schools for dance, music, photography, sculpture and painting. With more than 160 exhibition rooms, it is claimed as the most important cultural centre in Latin America.

Concerts are held in the main patio, which has featured singers such as Carrera and Pavarotti. The former kitchen is used now for banquets on state occasions, such as the visits of international statesmen or royalty, including Prince Philip.

But the great highlight is the series of ceiling paintings done by the muralist José Clemente Orozco in the desanctified chapel. The frescoes, completed in 1939, depict the agony of man in his experience of war and violence.

The great centrepiece is "The Man of Fire", which occupies the dome. These stark murals, covering the walls and ceiling, can give viewers a major crick in the neck. Wooden benches have been provided, so that visitors can view the paintings while lying down.

Afterwards, back in the Plaza again, test out the four bronze seats which show a highly imaginative approach to park bench design. This magic circle was the gift of an architect who wanted passers-by to experience modern sculpture, even if they didn't enter the Cultural Institute.

Shopping time

In total contrast, only a block or two away is the multi-storied **Liberty Market**, the biggest in Mexico. It has wide sections for shoes, leather, dresses, sombreros, flowers, fruit and children's toys. There's everything which local shoppers may require, from kitchenware to bananas or toothpaste. The central patio is richly colourful, with displays of tropical fruits. Above, restaurants offer all the local food specialities at prices geared to local incomes.

The market is right next to the **Plaza de Mariachis** which echoes every evening with bands that play the music born in Guadalajara: a combination of guitars, violins and trumpets. Musicians are dressed in black, with white shirts and flowing cravats. Piped trouser seams are studded with silver buttons. Larger groups perform for tourist parties, and have an elegance to their bearing. But smaller bands look rather seedy, as they stand around with battered intruments, hoping to be hired to play a tune or sing a song.

For a long-lasting memory of Mexico, that's where to go in the evening, perhaps after a stroll through the beautifully illuminated Historical Centre. Another alternative is a romantic horse-and-buggy ride. The white carriages are very charming with blue or yellow trimmings, and cost maybe £6 an hour to rent – but check the going rate before you embark.

If you're in Guadalajara during the October festival – which can stretch from about September 29 to November 5 – then every evening there are open-air music events, mostly free. The joyous atmosphere is part of the Mexican lifestyle.

Otherwise, another evening suggestion: take a cab to Tlaquepaque, for nightlife centred on **El Parián**. It's Mexico's biggest venue of its type, with capacity 2,000 people in 16 restaurants amd bars around a central patio and bandstand. The locals drink draught beer in quart-size goblets called a Chabela, which is also a girl's name.

Tlaquepaque

The towns of Tlaquepaque and Tonala, now part of metro Guadalajara, are famed for their hand-blown glass and painted ceramics, but they also produce a wider variety of quality giftware. With cobbled streets and colonial style architecture, Tlaquepaque's main avenue is pedestrianized with a comfortable pavement of bricks.

Craft and antique stores operate from elegant hacienda-type stately homes, with garden patios within. Most of the houses are late 17th and 18th-century. Visitors enjoy the combination of sightseeing and shopping on this popular half-day circuit from the centre of Guadalajara.

7.4 *Jalisco province*

To many people, the State of Jalisco – of which Guadalajara is the capital – embodies the soul of Mexico. It is home to many traditions and products most identified with Mexico. Tequila comes from this region, besides mariachi music and many of Mexico's traditional dishes. Jalisco also claims honours for creating the Mexican Hat Dance as well as the *charreada,* the Mexican rodeo. Jalisco is cowboy country.

Near Guadalajara, endless plantations of cactus-like blue agave surround the town of Tequila. Several distilleries offer tours and tastings. The agave grows for 8 to 12 years. Then the core of the plant, weighing from 100 to 150 kilos, is taken to the factory. After hot steaming and crushing, the pulp is put into big steel containers for fermentation, followed by distillation and ageing into tequila.

Continuing towards Puerto Vallarta, the road passes macabre lava fields in the region of Ixtlán del Rio. That is the fallout from the Volcano of El Ceboruca, which flung out debris twelve miles. The last eruption was in 1870. Closer to the coast there is tropical jungle vegetation, and big plantations of bananas and cacao.

Chapter Eight

Go shopping

Business hours

Mexican shopping hours are generally 9.30 or 10 till 9 in the evening, but stores close for siesta from 1 or 2 p.m. till 4 p.m. However, in Cancún's Hotel Zone the shopping malls take an American view of trading hours, shop till you drop.

If you haven't geared yourself to the Mexican siesta, then you can escape the afternoon sun into the air conditioned arcades. Sun sets around 5.30 p.m., beaches are vacated, and visitors can concentrate on serious shop-gazing.

Value Added Tax is 15%. Most outlets include VAT in the marked price – *IVA incluido*. Otherwise they should make it clear that IVA must be added.

What to buy

If you are desperate for a sombrero, or a warm blanket, or an Aztec idol carved in onyx, the widest possible choice awaits. Shops offer everything from designer fashions to casual resort wear, fine jewellery to hand-crafted leather goods, embroidered skirts and blouses to souvenir T-shirts.

Local handicrafts such as hand painted ceramics, silver, basketware, hammocks, colourful Mexican rugs, guitars and other musical instruments all make popular gifts and mementoes, at very reasonable prices.

Where to buy

Prices are best in the region of origin. That's a bonus for anyone touring the country and alert to the local production. Guadalajara, for instance, is great for a wide range of handicrafts; Mérida specialises in hammocks and embroidered blouses and tunic-style shirts; Taxco, on the road to Acapulco, has a big reputation for silverware.

Isla Mujeres is well known for high-fashion jewellery, sold by prestigious international firms such as Van Cleef & Arpels. Local craftsmen mount diamonds, emeralds, saphires, rubies and other precious and semi-precious stones into elegant settings.

In Cancún's hotel zone, every imaginable item is displayed in glitzy plazas such as Caracol, Mayfair, Kukulcán and Flamingo. Boutiques carry a full range of Mexican and foreign luxury goods, with fixed prices, no haggling. Smaller stores focus their sales pitch on discounts. A typical jeweller proclaims "Gold 30% discount – cheap as never before." It can seem like a bargain, but the original price has probably been set high, to compensate. When bargaining it's best to talk pesos, not dollars. Remember that credit card deals are liable to a 6% tax.

Haggling is the rule in what are described as Flea Markets. These sell only newly-made antiques, and traditional handicrafts that are new off the production line. At the Zócalo by the Convention Center in Cancún's Hotel Zone, two Flea Markets face one other. Identical articles are cheaper in Cancún town, in a group of charming little side streets just off Tulum Avenue. In Playa del Carmen, the main pedestrianised street running parallel to the coast – called Avenida 5A Norte – is lined with every style of shop, but you'll find lower prices in the side streets.

In Puerto Vallarta similar products are available along the Malecón (the city's waterfront walkway) and in the cobblestone side streets. There is good shopping for silver and gold.

71

Caution!

Some Cancún stores display products of black coral, which is banned from all civilised countries. Remember that it takes 50 years to grow a centimetre. Dedicated supporters of the environment will probably want to avoid any store that sells black coral.

Beach vendors peddle a full range of craft products, souvenirs, leather goods and sun-hats. But don't buy silver and gold on the beach, as there's no guarantee. If you later have doubts about authenticity, you may never see the vendor again.

Be careful about people outside the hotel (or even inside!) who offer a free breakfast or a heavily discounted tour. These philanthropists are not in the catering or tour business. Once you are captured, they will take up precious hours of your holiday in a time-share or condominium hard sell. There's no such thing as a free breakfast: it can cost the price of a time-share.

Prices for local spirits like tequila, rum or brandy are very cheap in supermarkets. Incidentally, Cancún – and indeed the whole state of Quintana Roo – is a duty-free zone. For bottles to take home, or Cuban cigars, it's not worth holding back for Duty Free at the airport, where choice is more limited and prices may not be lower. Likewise most of the airport giftware is higher priced and tatty.

Chapter Nine

Food and drink

9.1 Some like it hot

Mexican food is among the world's most interesting: a happy marriage of Aztec and Mayan cuisines – based on maize, beans, chillies, fruits, vegetables and game – with Spanish cuisine as an equal partner.

Just consider how many world foods have been introduced from the lands of Aztec and Maya: maize, cocoa, turkeys, vanilla, potatoes, tomatoes, pineapples, avocados, peanuts and squash.

Although there's wide-open choice in the resorts to eat any style from French haute cuisine down to American fast-food, it's worth sampling the Mexican kitchen as part of the holiday experience.

However, first a warning! An all-Mexican meal is often accompanied by three side dishes of sauces – choice of liquid red dynamite, green dynamite, and what looks like a very small salad of finely chopped onion and tomatoes. But that also is dynamite.

Like all forms of explosive, these products should be handled with extreme caution. If your stomach is not already battle-hardened by regular exposure to Mexican spices, there's the possibility of a 24-hour internal explosion.

The big stomach-buster is a very small green chilli called Habañero. Mexicans display their machismo by eating a couple raw at a sitting, but even a tiny taste can set your lips on fire.

Chilli diet

Each year the average Mexican family consumes more chilli peppers than onions or tomatoes. Vegetable markets display several dozen breeds of chilli, some looking like sweet and innocent paprikas.

Fortunately, many restaurants for gringos are Habañero-free zones, as they don't want to lose their customers for evermore. But it's always best to check. Dicing with *salsas* is always voluntary.

Not all the sauces are hot. A favourite ingredient is *tomate verde* (green tomato), which is not a true tomato but a small limegreen fruit. The tartness of the tomate verde blends well with onions, coriander and garlic, sometimes enriched with bits of avocado.

Beans with everything

If you like beans, Mexico is paradise. There are numerous varieties, cooked many ways, and appearing in sundry disguises from breakfast onwards.

A typical buffet breakfast can tempt you to load your plate with bacon fried so crisp that it splinters; fried or scrambled eggs; maybe a red sausage or two.

But also take a dollop of something that looks like chocolate pudding. It's *frijoles refritos* – refried beans – a great Mexican speciality, made of boiled brown beans mashed and then fried with a little spice. They resurface with many other dishes and are a key filling for tacos.

Beans also appear in many hearty soups and stews and main courses. There's a black bean soup made with ham and vegetables. Or try a main course of *frijoles charros* – cowboy-style beans with bacon, sausage and vegetables.

Mexican patriots eat *bandera de frijoles*, different-coloured beans with stewed pork, red peppers, cheese and avocado to represent the red, white and green of the national flag.

Tortilla country

Equally basic to Mexican eating is the tortilla, which has nil connection with Spain's omelettes. These thin flat pancakes have been rolled out as corn meal paste since early Indian times, and are cooked on a griddle. In the villages they are still hand made.

Town dwellers now buy their tortillas from a bakery, where the end product comes streaming off a conveyor belt, to be piled high on the shop scales and sold by weight. An average family eats two kilos a day.

Mexican restaurants serve them automatically, usually stacked in a covered basket to keep warm. The technique is to hold a tortilla in one hand, spread some sauce to enliven the flat taste, and load with bits of meat and vegetables from your plate. Then fold into an envelope, or roll it up like a fat cigar, and you have a do-it-yourself taco.

Tortillas are also used as the ground base for fried or scrambled eggs with onions and tomatoes – and beans, of course – plus chilli for those who like fire in their belly. Often tortillas appear as a crispy side dish; or they are limply fried and rolled around great choice of fillings to make *enchiladas* – turkey, cheese, eggs, beans, pork, you-name-it but beware of lurking chillies. If wheat flour is used, they are called *burritos*.

Mealtimes

Start the day any time till noon with a hearty Mexican breakfast from your hotel buffet. If you're on a room-only arrangement, numerous outside restaurants offer all-you-can-eat breakfast deals for $5 or $6.

Orange juice has all the genuine flavour of being freshly pressed. If you like tea, bring your favourite tea-bags. But the Mexican home-grown coffee is excellent. Try a plate of fresh fruit – papaya, water melon, sweet melon, pineapple, peach and banana.

Lunches heavy or fast

Many restaurants also feature buffet lunches at eye-catching low prices. For most Mexicans, lunch is the heaviest meal of the day, starting at 2 p.m. and finishing with siesta. Dinner is from 8 p.m. To stave off hunger in between, Mexican towns have fast-food stalls at every street corner, selling *tamales, tacos, enchiladas* and *burritos*. There is great culinary scope for the adventurous. Enjoy your meal – *¡Buen provecho!*

9.2 Regional specialities

Mexico offers a wide range of regional cuisines. Obviously seaside areas specialise in fish. A typical beachside restaurant in the Puerto Vallarta area features lobster, octopus, shrimp and red snapper. Shrimp can be prepared in many ways: as a kebab with beef; rolled in bacon; breaded; or cooked with garlic. Don't order lobster without checking the price first.

Otherwise, the cuisine of Jalisco State – which includes Guadalajara and Puerto Vallarta – is best known for its crisp fried pork *carnitas*; and a stew called *pozole*. It is the home of tequila, fried tacos and red-chilli enchiladas. Here's a check-list of local dishes to sample – or avoid!

Birria is made from diced beef, with garlic, onions, laurel leaves, cumin, and chilli to taste.
Pozole is a highly popular stew with pork, hominy, red chilli and garlic. It can be garnished with sliced radish, lettuce, oregano and onion. But there's no way of dodging the chilli.
Mole is a combination of several different chillies, simmered with chicken, pork or turkey. Its basic ferocity is curbed by adding chocolate.
Torta ahogada – a long roll or baguette, slit open to accommodate pork or other meat, with lettuce, tomato, onion, cheese and green peppers. Mexicans take it as a hangover cure, plunging the torta into a very hot sauce. The cure could be even worse than staying with the hangover.

Call of the Yucatán

In the Yucatán Peninsula, the cuisine mirrors its Mayan origins. From pork in banana leaves to chicken with vinegar and spices and the famed *achiote* chili sauce, this region's specialities are among the most unusual in Mexico.

Pescado Yucatán – a fish fillet of snapper, marinated with achiote sauce and wrapped in banana leaves; served with rice and vegetables.

Sopa de Lima – a thick soup of shredded chicken, vegetable, fragments of fried tortilla and flavoured with lime juice. Don't miss it!

Huevos motuleños – an enormous breakfast dish of refried beans and a fried egg, topped with peas, chopped ham and grated cheese and covered in tomato sauce – all sitting on a tortilla base. Slices of fried banana can also enter the picture. It could equally serve as a main course for lunch or dinner.

Pollo pibil – chicken marinated in achiote chilli sauce, peppercorns, cumin, garlic, salt and sour orange juice. For added flavour and to retain the juices, it is baked and served in a banana leaf. Despite the trace of achiote chilli sauce, it is not spicy, and is certainly worth trying.

Cochinita pibil – same as pollo pibil, but made with pork instead of chicken.

Poc-chuc – sliced pork marinated in sour orange juice, served with pickled onions and a zippy sauce.

Puchero – just about everything goes into this stew of pork, chicken, with banana and any handy vegetables like cabbage, squash, carrots, potatoes and yams; garnished with radish and sour orange juice.

Frijoles con puerco – diced pork with black beans, and eaten with rice.

Salbutes – fried tortillas served with shredded turkey, slices of avocado and pickled onion.

Pavo escabeche – another variation of shredded turkey, soaked in a spicy sauce.

9.3 All the drinks

Mexico is a haven for inexpensive beers and liquors, from the national drink of tequila to Mexican versions of rum, brandy and Cointreau. Downtown supermarket prices are very low, even for the somewhat more expensive wines from Baja California in northwest Mexico.

Tequila comes from a town of the same name, near Guadalajara; and Mexico is the only country in the world which produces this alcohol derived from the juice of the blue maguey plant.

Most Mexicans drink it straight. They put a little salt on their hand, gulp the hard stuff in one slug, and follow with the salt and a squeeze of lemon or lime as a chaser.

Otherwise, tequila can be mixed with various fruit juices or soda pops, including a local brand called Squirt.

Cocktail country

Numerous cocktails are available. Some are rum-based, such as Planters Punch, Piña Colada, Cuba Libre (rum and Coke) or Daiquiri (with strawberry, sweet melon, water melon and bananas). Desarmador is better known to gringos as a Screwdriver, vodka and orange juice.

A Margarita is made from tequila, with lemon and crushed ice. Often it is served in huge goblets, keeping you more than happy during Happy Hour, two for the price of one.

For a sundowner, a Tequila Sunset is appropriate; or possibly a Tequila Sunrise when a nightspot is calling for last orders.

Another popular thirst-quencher is Coco loco – a coconut, scalped, a couple of straws, and you drink the milk which is laced with tequila, rum, vodka, gin and brandy, maybe with added grenadine or pineapple juice.

Many bars offer their own cocktail specials with tempting names. What male could refuse a Foolish Virgin, a mixture of golden rum, cointreau and tropical fruit juice?

Flaming cockroach

A fun drink in the Yucatán is cucaracha, meaning cockroach. It's a straight liquor which they ignite. You drink it through a straw while it's burning with a blue flame. Anyone who drinks three of them will be on his back under the table, like a drunken cockroach.

Somewhat less potent are numerous brands of beer, though canned beer carries the small-print message 'Excessive consumption of this product is harmful to health.' Among the best known brands are Sol, Corona, Tecate and Dos Equis, but the lesser known labels such as the Guinness-type Negro Modelo or Negro Especial can be every bit as good.

Wines of the country

European wine imports are expensive, so it's worth trying the Mexican product. The principal name in the business is Pedro Domecq, with their red and white Celafia brands. The red is particularly good, mellow and smooth, comparable to a quality Spanish red. The white Celafia, when well chilled, is crisp and very similar to a Soave. Many bars feature Sangria.

Among the soft drinks, there's the usual choice of Coke or Pepsi. But there's more local character in freshly squeezed orange juice, or carrot, mango or papaya – all sold by street vendors with a tricycle cart.

Chapter Ten

Quick facts

Terrain
The central highlands, comprising 60% of the country's land mass, are enclosed to the east and west by the Sierra Madre Oriental and Sierra Madre Occidental mountain ranges; and to the south by towering, widely spaced volcanoes. The low-lying Yucatán Peninsula is bordered by Guatamala and Belize.

Natural resources: petroleum, silver, copper, gold, lead, zinc, natural gas, timber
Population: 96 million
Population growth rate: 1.94%
Life expectancy: 72.94 years
Total fertility rate: 3.17 children per woman
Ethnic divisions: mestizo (Indian-Spanish) 60%, Amerindian 30%, Caucasian 9%
Religions: nominally Roman Catholic 89%, Protestant 6%
Languages: Spanish, various Mayan dialects
Literacy: 87% age 15 and over can read and write
Labour force: 26.2 million
By occupation: services 31.7%, agriculture, forestry, hunting, and fishing 28%, commerce 14.6%, manufacturing 11.1%, construction 8.4%, transport 4.7%, mining and quarrying 1.5%
Government: Federal republic operating under a centralized government.

Economy overview

Mexico's economy is beginning to rebound from the economic difficulties of the 1980s but still faces many key challenges. During the 1980s, the accumulation of large external debts, falling oil prices, prices, rapid population growth, and mounting inflation and unemployment plagued the economy.

The government has responded with sweeping economic reforms. Many state enterprises have been privatized, including all of the commercial banks. Strict fiscal and monetary discipline have reduced inflation, which still hovers near 30%. However, the tight money policies have restricted growth.

Aimed at boosting trade and investment, the North American Free Trade Agreement (NAFTA) with the United States and Canada came into force in January 1994. Despite the prospects of long-term gains under NAFTA, Mexico still faces difficult problems, including unemployment, continuing social inequalities, and increased trade competition.

Exports: crude oil and oil products, coffee, silver, engines, motor vehicles, cotton, consumer electronics.

Industries: food and beverages, tobacco, chemicals, iron and steel, petroleum, mining, textiles, clothing, motor vehicles, consumer durables, tourism.

Agriculture: accounts for 9% of GDP and over 25% of work force, with large number of small farms at subsistence level. Major food crops – maize, wheat, rice, beans. Cash crops – cotton, coffee, fruit, tomatoes.

Chapter Eleven

Looking at the past

Origins

50,000 BC The first inhabitants of the Americas arrive from Asia, crossing an ice bridge which then linked Siberia and Alaska across the Bering Straits. The nomads spread south.

12,000 BC The oldest human remains found in Mexico.

3,000 BC The beginning of maize cultivation, with beans and squash.

1800-200 BC: Preclassical Period

Communities are based on fishing, hunting and gathering, with simple agriculture. Some towns become ceremonial centres, with fertility worship. These settlements arise in several regions of Mesoamerica – that is the area stretching from present-day Tampico and Mazatlán in the north, to the border of Honduras.

The Olmecs create the earliest culture, ranging from 1200 to 175 BC in the present-day states of Veracruz and Tabasco. A Monte Albán community is established about 700 BC; Teotihuacán around 300 BC, with building of first pyramids.

200 BC to 900 AD: Classical Period

The high point of urban life, and the formation of powerful priest cultures. Maximum development of Mesoamerican civilization and overall consolidation of skills in art, ceramics, literature and astronomy. Some cities rise, others fall.

The Mayas establish a wide-spread jungle civilisation from 150 to 900 AD. Splendid cities develop at Teotihuacán, Monte Albán, Uxmal, Palenque, Tajín, Cobá, Bonampak, Yaxchilán.

900 to 1521 AD: Post-Classical Period
The theocratic societies become militarized as metal-working develops. The warlike Toltecs reach their peak development in Tula. They invade Mayan territory in the Yucatán, and establish a capital at Chichén Itzá, evolving a joint Mayan-Toltec culture.

1325 The foundation of Tenochtitlán (today's Mexico City) by the Aztecs. Believing the world had already been destroyed four times, they try to save the Fifth Universe from destruction by appeasing the gods with human sacrifices. They need frequent wars to ensure a supply of victims. The Aztecs become mighty, but unpopular.

1517 Exploratory expedition of Hernández de Córdova along the Yucatán coast.

1518 Juan de Grijalva sails along the Mexican coast, from Cozumel to Cabo Roxo, collecting the first European impression of Mesoamerican grandeur. Population is estimated at 25 million.

April 1519 Hernán Cortés founds the first Spanish settlement in Mexico called La Villa Rica de la Vera Cruz. He scuttles his ships to prevent mutiny or desertion and marches inland.

Nov 1519 The Spaniards arrive in Tenochtitlán. Móctezuma II gives a peaceful welcome and invites them to stay in the Palace of Axayácatl. Cortés then takes Móctezuma prisoner.

1520 Cortés departs on other business, leaving a garrison in charge. While Cortés is away, an Aztec festival ends with the massacre of 200 Aztec nobles and the death of Móctezuma. Later, the Spanish retreat, but many are killed.

May 1521 The Spaniards return, tear down outer Aztec fortifications, and besiege the city.

August 1521 Tenochtitlán falls, and the Aztec empire comes to a sudden end.

The Colonial Period

1522-1536 A series of expeditions expand the territory under Spanish control. Tenochtitlán is razed, renamed Mexico and rebuilt as the capital of New Spain. Franciscan monks arrive, followed by Dominicans and then Augustinians.

1600 By the turn of the century, the native population has been reduced mainly by European diseases to a mere 1.5 million. Some 250 monasteries and convents have been built.

1692 Riot in Mexico City. The crowd sets fire to the Viceroyal Palace and City Hall.

1700-1800 New Spain doubles in area, thanks to military expeditions and the work of missionaries. Many immigrants arrive from Spain, and there is much intermarriage. Rich silver mines bring great prosperity to landowners and the middle classes. The French Revolution and the American War of Independence stir a similar yearning among the settlers for self-government, breaking loose from Spain.

1810-1821 The War for Independence. The priest Miguel Hidalgo gives the shout for independence in Dolores, takes up the flag of the Virgen of Guadalupe and leads a mob-style army.

1811 Loyalists rout the insurgents. Rebel leaders are captured, and sentenced to death for treason. But the struggle continues under the leadership of Father Morelos.

Post-Independence Mexico

1821 After a decade of struggle, Mexico achieves independence, with the triumphant arrival of Agustín de Iturbide in Mexico City. Iturbide reigns briefly as Emperor of Mexico, until the monarchy is dissolved and a federal republic established on the US model.

1845 USA annexes Texas.

1846-1848 Mexico launches a war against the United States, ending in a treaty ceding Texas, New Mexico and California to USA for a payment of $18,250,000.

1858-1861 A War for Reform erupts between Liberals and Conservatives.

1859 The Reform Laws feature Nationalization of Church property; Civil Marriages; Secularization of Cemeteries; Freedom of Worship.

1862 Conservatives ally themselves to the French who send troops to Mexico City. The liberal government is deposed.

1864 The Second Empire. An Austrian archduke, Maximilian Hapsburg, is named the Emperor of Mexico. Maximilian signs a Treaty with Napoleon III, in which the latter promises to pay the high expenses of intervention in return for which Maximilian must follow the policies set by Napoleon.

1867 The French neglect Maximilian, and withdraw their troops. Maximilian wants to abdicate, but the Conservatives persuade him to continue. Centred on Querétaro, he is constantly attacked by republican forces. Finally the Liberals capture Maximilian and he is shot by firing squad. The Republic is re-established with Benito Juárez as President.

The Porfiriata

1876-1911 General Porfirio Díaz is elected President and takes a tight grip on power, while bringing economic prosperity. His 30 years in uninterrupted office contrasts with the 30 years from 1821 to 1850 which saw fifty changes of government. He brings maximum exploitation of mineral and petroleum resources, carries out important public works projects and attracts foreign investment.

1908 Díaz declares in an interview with an American journalist that his successor should emerge through a political party structure, in a fair and open election. These words spark the creation of parties opposed to his dictatorship.

1910 Francisco Madero publishes a revolutionary plan for effective suffrage, with a special clause to prohibit the President from being re-elected.

The Revolution

1910 Armed rebellion finally tumbles President Díaz from power.

1911 Emiliano Zapata calls for agrarian reforms and backs his message with the slogan *tierra y libertad* - land and freedom. Madero becomes President.

1913 The Conservative opposition, backed by USA, stages a coup. Madero is assassinated.

1917 The new constitution is announced and Venustiano Carranza is elected the new constitutional President.

1919 Emiliano Zapata is assassinated.

Post-revolutionary Mexico

1920 After ten years of civil war, there follows a period of relative peace and reform.

1926 During the presidency of Plutarco Elías Calles, the Cristero Revolt erupts. The archbishop of Mexico is arrested for declaring that the clergy will not recognize and will fight anticlerical articles of the constitution. But the revolt is put down, priests are executed, and church power in state affairs is eradicated.

1929 Formation of the first official political party, the Partido Nacional Revolucionario (currently the Partido Revolucionario Institucional).

1938 President Lázaro Cárdenas decrees the expropriation of petroleum companies and the foundation of the Compania Exportadora del Petroleo Nacional. Control of the national rail system is handed over to the rail-workers' union a year after nationalization.

1968 Olympic Games held in Mexico City, but preceded by strong student and working-class riots against the one-party state.

1982 President José López Portillo nationalizes banks.

1986 The collapse of petroleum prices is among a number of factors causing economic problems. Mexico enters GATT (General Agreement on Tariffs and Trade).

Chapter Twelve

Learn some Spanish

Spanish is the official language of Mexico, though more than fifty local languages are spoken by 25% of the population. In the Yucatán, for instance, villagers of Maya descent still speak their own mother tongue, based on the original language from 2,000 years ago. It's not taught in schools but passed down the generations.

But still everyone speaks Spanish, though most people in tourism can cope with English. However, there's pleasure in being able to use and recognise even just a few words of Spanish.

Your waiter's usual friendly greeting is "¡Hola amigo!" It's nice to make the same response, or beat him to it. Some club hotels include a basic daily lesson in their activities programme – a kind of mental aerobics.

Certainly some Spanish is helpful when venturing beyond your resort. If you are self-driving in more off-trail areas, it's useful to carry a pocket phrase-book.

If you already know Spanish, be prepared for a few adjustments. In mainland Spain, 'c' before 'i' or 'e' is pronounced like 'th' in 'think'. *Cinco* is pronounced 'thinko' in Spain, but 'sinko' in Mexico. In Spain, 'z' is pronounced 'th', but always 's' in Latin America.

Also, many Latin American words are quite different from European Spanish. A car is *un carro*, while *un charro* is a Mexican cowboy or it could be a sombrero.

Spanish is helpful in making only one sound for each vowel. Here's the pronunciation code:

a is like the short a in English father.
e is like the short e in bed
i is like the long e in see
o is like the short o in off
u is like the English oo in boot.

Don't worry about the accents. Apart from ñ (pronounced as in onion), the accents merely indicate the syllable to stress. Otherwise they don't change the vowel sound. Here's a starter kit of a few words to show you're trying.

Greetings

Hello	hola
Goodbye	bye-bye
Good morning	buenos dias
Good afternoon	buenas tardes
Good evening	buenas noches
How are you?	¿cómo está usted?
Very well, thanks	muy bien, gracias

General

Yes	sí
No	no
Please	por favor
Thank you	gracias
Do you speak English?	¿habla inglés?
I don't understand	no comprendo
What time is it?	¿qué hora es?

Sightseeing

Where is ...?	¿Donde esta... ?
the beach	la playa
the church	la iglesia
the museum	el museo
the port	el puerto
the square	la plaza; el zócalo
the station	la estación
the street	la calle
the seafront promenade	el malecón

Shopping

Bank	banco
Currency exchange	cambio
Chemist	farmacia
Hairdresser	peluqueria
Supermarket	supermercado
Tobacconist	estanco
Post office	correos
Stamps	timbre
Postcard	postal
How much is it?	¿cuanto es?

Signs

Abierto	open
Ascensor	lift/elevator
Baño damas	ladies' WC
Baño hombres	gents WC
Caliente	hot
Cerrado	shut
Empujar	push
Entrada	entrance
Frío	cold
Libre	vacant
Parada de autobús	bus stop
Parada de taxis	cab rank
Prohibido entrar	no entrance
Prohibido fumar	no smoking
Salida	exit
Salida de emergencia	emergency exit

Numbers

0-10 cero, uno, dos, tres, cuatro, cinco, seis, siete, ocho, nueve, diez
11-19 once, doce, trece, catorce, quince, dieciseis, diecisiete, dieciocho, diecinueve
20-29 veinte, veintiuno, veintidos, veintetres etc.
30-39 treinta, treinta y uno, treinta y dos, etc.
40, 50...-90 – cuaranta, cincuenta, sesenta, setenta, ochenta, noventa
100 cien/ciento; 101 ciento uno; 200 doscientos.
500 quinientos; 1000 mil; 2000 dos mil;
1,000,000   un millón

Chapter Thirteen

Travel tips

13.1 Transport

Mexico is a land of big distances, and walking won't take you very far. Resort hotels are spread along miles of waterfront. However, buses are built to serve holiday guests. They are very frequent, with low one-price fares for any distance.

Taxis are not metered except in Mexico City, but set prices are charged on a zonal system. Their rates are reasonable, and most cabbies understand English.

Car hire is an option for day trips, especially for travellers who want to sample off-trail beaches. But night travel can be nerve-racking, especially when truck drivers are competing for the same stretch of highway. There are very steep cambers, and ditches on either side.

Reckon about 45 dollars a day for a VW Beetle; 60 to 70 for a Nissan with air conditioning; and 70 to 75 dollars a day for a jeep. Petrol costs under £1 per imperial gallon. You can do about 350 miles on a full tank costing around £10. Filling stations are few and far between, so keep your tank topped up.

First-class buses on longer journeys offer speedy and air-conditioned transport at remarkably low cost. Forget all those funny stories about Latin disregard for time-keeping! These buses operate on precise schedules, departing exactly on the minute. For a small saving of money, it's not worth choosing the second-class buses, which are slower, with more stops and detours, but more cheerfully ethnic. All buses are non-smoking, by law.

Train travel? Don't bother unless you're a dedicated rail buff.

Air travel: the principal domestic airlines – Aeroméxico and Mexicana – operate frequent services, mainly using Mexico City as the hub. Aeroméxico, for instance, averages six flights a day from Cancún to the capital, or three or four daily flights from Puerto Vallarta. That's in addition to scheduled services with major US cities.

A determined sightseer could visit most of the sites and cities described in this book, by a combination of buses, tour coaches and airline connections such as Mérida/Mexico City/Guadalajara to Puerto Vallarta and back to Cancún.

13.2 Tipping

In Mexico, tipping is a national sport. Workers in the service industries depend on 10 or 15% to augment their nominal basic wage. A key phrase on restaurant bills is *'Propina no incluida'* – Tip not included. However, a few restaurants do add a service charge. If in doubt, check.

On sightseeing trips, the driver and guide appreciate a dollar or two, which they usually share. For porters, reckon 50 US cents per bag. It is not customary to tip cab drivers.

Many 'all-inclusive' hotels follow a no-tipping policy. It's all covered in the holiday cost. If, however, your favourite waiter or chambermaid has always done a really nice friendly job, then a gesture of appreciation is not out of line. But there's no obligation. If in doubt, ask guidance from your travel-agency rep.

If you think of making a gift of oddments like toiletries which you don't want to carry back home, then write and sign a covering note. The staff are very honest. But, as part of hotel security, staff are liable to be searched to ensure nothing leaves the premises without permission.

13.3 Electricity

The current is 110 volts, 60 cycles, as in USA and Canada. Any gadgets you bring must be switcheable to that voltage. You should also take an adaptor, as Mexico uses flat two-pin American style plugs.

There are no adaptors locally available which can adapt from UK 3-pin. Suitable adaptors are available in UK department stores, such as Woolworths, Boots and Dixons; and also at the departure airport.

Re-check that your adaptor has two flat pins that plug into the wall socket, and three slots for your British appliance. Continental adaptors with round pins will not work in Mexico.

13.4 Mexican time

Most of Mexico – in all the areas covered in this book – is 6 hours behind GMT and 7 hours behind British Summer Time. In North American terms, it's on Central Standard Time.

The exception is Nuevo Vallarta, which is just across the State boundary into Mountain Standard Time. In practice, because of proximity to Puerto Vallarta, hotels in Nuevo Vallarta keep to Central Time.

13.5 Phoning and writing home

Think twice before phoning home from your hotel. Typical cost is £20 for a 3-minute minimum call to UK. Carefully check the pricing rules before making the call, as the charges can vary greatly from hotel to hotel.

Some hotels will ask for a credit card imprint before opening the line to a client's room to permit direct dialling. The shock then comes at the end of the holiday.

A second option is to go down to reception, give them the number, make the call and pay for it immediately. If you then feel bitten, at least you'll be twice shy.

Phone card

The least expensive option is to use the Telmex/Ladatel card in a public call box. Buy a 50-peso card which will give about 3 minutes' conversation and then cut off. You'll probably then still have 11 pesos left on the card, but not enough to pay for another minute of international time. You can use the remainder on local calls, costing only half a peso for each 22 minutes.

The direct-dialling code to call the U.K. is 98 + 44 + the STD area code omitting the zero, followed by the local number. For USA and Canada, dial 98 + 1 + area code etc.

A mini-problem is that phone cards can be elusive to buy. Some hotel desks sell them, but supermarkets are more likely.

Public phone and fax kiosks offer another route for international calls. But, despite what fancy discounts the operators may advertise, you'll still pay twice as much as by Telecard.

Likewise a fax can come expensive. A typical one-pager sent to an automatic fax receiver may take 57 seconds to transmit, or possibly 62 seconds. Typically you could pay £3 for the first minute; but twice as much if transmission goes for a single second into the next minute.

Sending a letter or postcard? To reach Britain will take anything from ten days to infinity.

13.6 Newspapers, radio & TV

Most hotel satellite TV's give you local Spanish-language programmes, news by courtesy of CNN, and maybe other US channels. The visitor from UK can feel very cut off from more important home news such as the cricket scores.

It's worth travelling with a short-wave radio, to pick up the regular on-the-hour news bulletins of the BBC World Service. Reception varies according to time and location, and can always be improved if you take a length of aerial wire to dangle from your hotel window.

Try the following wave-lengths:

Morning is best for Voice of America on 9590 kHz or 9760; for BBC try 11750, especially for News from Britain at 6.15 local time; or 9740.

Evening is best on 5975 or 7325; or 9915; or Euronews on 9740.

Mexico City News is the English-language daily, but the cover price is increased outside the capital. *Newsweek* and *Time* are on sale a day after publication. Some US newspapers are available, but UK publications are very rare.

13.7 Security

Anywhere in Cancun or Puerto Vallarta is very safe, with minimal risk of getting mugged, whether in the Hotel Zone areas or downtown. Just take elementary precautions against pickpockets in crowded market areas.

Late at night it's sensible to use a taxi and avoid carrying large sums of money.

Mexico is a low-risk country for holiday-makers and their valuables. A cautious policy is to put traveller cheques, jewellery, passport and return ticket into a hotel room safe or in the safe deposit at reception.

However, the chance of theft is low, especially in the all-inclusive hotels which control entry at the perimeter gate. Anyway, there's no need to carry passport and tickets around. The problems are enormous if these items are mislaid, causing a great waste of holiday time.

13.8 Photo hints

In the brilliant tropical sunshine, slowish films around ASA 100 will give good results for colour prints. Concentrate your picture-making on early morning or late afternoon.

Noontime sun makes people squint, and strong light on beaches casts very harsh shadows. Also, the midday sun gives too much glare, though a lens hood and a polarization filter can help overcome the problem.

Sunset watching

Towards evening, dusk is very brief. Capture that sunset picture quickly, before it disappears! Make your beach photos more interesting with a foreground tree as a frame or silhouette.

Fine sand on the lens can be a nuisance. Keep the lens cap in place, whenever the camera is not in use. To protect the lens, it's worth leaving a skylight filter permanently in place – much less costly to renew if over-vigorous cleaning causes scratches. Don't leave your camera lying in the sun, as heat can harm the film.

In the principal tourist locations, local people are accustomed to visiting shutterbugs with their desire to point cameras in every direction. Elsewhere, folk may be less tolerant of any invasion of their privacy.

However, if you don't make a big production of it, you can still get colourful shots of people in characteristic activity. Position yourself by a monument or in a crowded market, or at a crossroads. With a wide-angle lens for close-up, or long-focus lens for more distant shots, you can discreetly get all your local-colour pictures without irritating anyone. Take flash for pictures of evening activities and Mexican fiesta shows.

Film prices are elastic, depending where you buy. Often they cost more than in Britain or USA, so take plenty. If you use a specialised film, rather than standard brands, then take an over-supply. Off-beat films are hard to find.

Keep a note of photos taken, and their sequence. Otherwise, back home, it can be very difficult to identify every picture.

If you are planning to snorkel or scuba-dive, consider the purchase of an under-water camera to capture the beauty of the marine life and coral reefs. These cameras are available in resort, but are maybe cheaper if bought in Britain or USA.

There's a charge of 25 pesos for one day's use of a video camera at archaeological sites, but nothing to pay for still cameras.

13.9 Festivals and public holidays

An estimated 4,000 fiestas, festivals and holidays enliven Mexico each year. Some, like Easter, Independence Day, Christmas and the Day of the Dead, are celebrated everywhere. Others may occur only in one small village honouring its patron saint or a local historical event.

Some special foods appear only on certain holidays. Most holidays and festivals include a Mexican rodeo and a traditional marketplace, where local crafts, clothing and food provide nonstop temptation. No Mexican celebration is complete without fireworks.

While national holidays and other major events have fixed dates, local celebrations may vary. When in Mexico, check locally. A festival is always worth a special journey.

Official holidays

Jan 01 New Year's Day
Feb 05 Mexican Constitution Day
Mar 21 Birthday of President Benito Juárez
Mar/Apr Easter
May 01 Labour Day
May 05 Anniversary of Battle of Puebla in 1862
Sep 01 Annual State of the Union address given by the President
Sep 16 Independence Day
Oct 12 Columbus Day
Nov 01/02 All Saints Day: The Day of the Dead
Nov 20 Anniversary of the 1910 Revolution
Dec 12 Festival of Our Lady of Guadalupe
Dec 25 Christmas Day

13.10 Mexican Tourism Offices

London – 60/61 Trafalgar Square, WC2N 5DS. Tel: 0171-734-1058.
New York – Suite 1401, 405 Park Ave, NY 10022. Tel: 755-7261.
Toronto – Suite 1801, 2 Bloor St West, M4W 3E2. Tel: 925-0704.